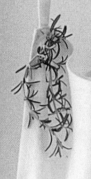

Sunset

complete home
storage

by Barbara J. Braasch and Lisa Stockwell Kessler ■ Sunset Books, Menlo Park, California

contents

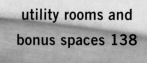

entryways 16

gathering places 28

bathrooms 106

home offices 122

outdoor and garden storage 166

SUNSET BOOKS

V.P., General Manager:
Richard A. Smeby
V.P., Editorial Director: Bob Doyle
Production Director: Lory Day
Operations Director:
Rosann Sutherland
Retail Sales Development Manager:
Linda Barker
Art Director: Vasken Guiragossian

Staff for this book:

Managing Editor: Claudia Blaine
Senior Editor, Sunset Books:
Bridget Biscotti Bradley
Writers: Barbara J. Braasch,
Lisa Stockwell Kessler
Art Director: Amy Gonzalez
Copy Editor: Elissa Rabellino
Photography Director and Stylist:
Cynthia Del Fava
Stylist: Jill Slater
Illustrator: Tracy La Rue Hohn
Page Production: Linda Bouchard
Woodworking Projects:
Fred Sotcher
Photo Research: Kimberly Parsons
Prepress Coordinator:
Eligio Hernandez
Proofreader: Peggy Gannon
Indexer: Nanette Cardon

Cover photography by Luca Trovato

10 9 8 7 6 5 4 3
First printing June 2003
Copyright © 2003 Sunset Publishing
Corporation, Menlo Park, CA 94025.
Second edition. All rights reserved,
including the right of reproduction in
whole or in part in any form.

ISBN: 0-376-01770-8
Library of Congress Control Number:
2003103841
Printed in the United States.

For additional copies of *Complete Home
Storage* or any other Sunset book,
call 1-800-526-5111 or visit us at
www.sunset.com.

chapter one

getting organized

Where are the keys? Has anyone seen the dog's leash? Did you find last month's magazine? Are there any clean towels? Where is my favorite sweater (or CD, or book bag)? If these last-minute domestic crises sound all too familiar, take heart; there's an easier way to live.

All it involves is getting—and staying—organized, and that's something you learned in kindergarten.

The teacher always said, "Put it back where you found it, and you'll know where it is the next time you want it." Proper storage is integral to getting organized. So take a look at your possessions, get rid of what you don't need or absolutely love, and set up storage systems for the rest that work for your family.

Throughout this book you'll find loads of smart ideas, room-by-room storage solutions for your home and garden, and eight storage projects to build. The bonus? Once your home is clutter-free, you'll have more time for the things that really matter in life. For a list of retailers and manufacturers that specialize in organizing and storage products, turn to page 188.

corralling clutter

It's one of those age-old mysteries. No matter what the size of your home, your possessions will eventually expand to fill it. When that once-neat house starts overflowing with clutter, you have only two options: move to a larger place or figure out clever ways to create additional storage space for things worth keeping.

LIGHTEN UP

Regardless of how many things you have or closets you don't, the trick to being organized is lightening your load and deciding where to put what's left. Less is more, so keep only those things you now use, you will definitely use in the future, or that are of value to your family. Get rid of the rest.

PURGE Separating trash from treasure is difficult, so don't plan to organize the whole house, or even a room, in a day. Choose one area, work without distractions, and set a time limit, including time to clean up when you finish. You'll feel a sense of accomplishment when you're done, so reward yourself with a bubble bath, a latte, or a glass of wine.

Examine each item and make a decision to store it away, give it away, or throw it away. Don't agonize over items you're uncertain about; place them in a separate pile. At the end of the allotted time, stash them in a box, label and date it, and stow it away. If you haven't searched through the contents after a year, it's time to donate the box to charity.

MERGE Take a last look at throwaways before you toss them in the trash. Others may need the clothes that have hung unworn in your closet for a year or more, read those dog-eared books, use the too-small baby clothes, and enjoy the unused sports equipment and toys. So hold a garage sale, take items to a consignment shop, or donate them to a worthy cause.

SPLURGE ON STORAGE Half the job of organizing is having the right tools. Fortunately, there is a wide choice of storage products to help you organize your pared-down possessions. You may even find containers already at hand. Unused suitcases, hatboxes, decorative tins, and wicker baskets hide clutter, collect like items, and contribute to a room's decor.

Getting organized is not a onetime fix, so you'll occasionally need to check on how your storage systems are working. Just think of each shelf, drawer, cabinet, or closet as a plant that needs regular care to look its best.

donating

GETTING ORGANIZED MEANS disposing of what you no longer need, want, or use. If family or friends don't need your purged possessions, consider recycling them through charities such as Goodwill Industries, the Salvation Army, the St. Vincent de Paul Society, Vietnam Veterans of America, and Doctors without Borders. You'll help a worthy cause and receive a tax deduction. Other options are local churches, homeless shelters, disaster-relief organizations, and foreign-aid programs. Trash what's truly useless carefully, with as little damage to the environment as possible.

places for everything

There is no one way to store your belongings. Finding storage systems and routines that fit your lifestyle will minimize clutter and make the best use of your space. If you regularly drop your keys on an entry table, for instance, don't try to change that habit. Just add a container for keys, glasses, mail, or whatever else piles up there. But be careful that the container doesn't become a clutter collector; weed it periodically.

You can have as many possessions as you want—dozens of shoes or stacks of photos—but store them in ways that let you retrieve them when needed. Professional organizers will tell you that if you have to search for everything you store, your possessions own you rather than the other way around.

DIVIDE TO CONQUER

After your possessions have been pruned, organize them into four categories: easy access, display, concealed, and long term. Keep things you use or wear at least monthly within view and easy reach. Display cherished objects by collecting and creatively exhibiting them. Keep clutter under wraps by hiding it in drawers, cupboards, and closed cabinets. Relegate belongings used only seasonally or less, such as ski gear and holiday decorations, to long-term storage on hard-to-reach shelves, in the back of closets, or in labeled boxes in the attic, basement, or garage.

A SPACE SEARCH

Make an inventory of what you need to store: Count and measure every
item on every shelf and counter, and inside each drawer, container, and
closet. Note lost storage spaces, too, such as room between shelves that
could be retrofitted for better use. Once you figure how much space your
belongings need and what space is available, you know how much more
storage is required.

Expand every room's potential by adding storage to "invisible" spaces:
in hallways and corners, underneath stairs, behind doors, and around
windows. You can exhibit artwork and store valuable items in recessed
nooks between wall studs; house libraries in recessed areas beside stair-
cases; and display decorative or useful objects on shallow shelves above
kitchen sinks or behind doors.

storage systems

Efficient storage can blend into a room unobtrusively. You can create a look to coordinate with any decor and budget, whether units are retail or custom-built. A contemporary and inexpensive modular system (below) may be a perfect match for a casual family room, while a handsome albeit costly built-in (right) may add unexpected elegance to any space.

OPTIONS

Storage furniture is either freestanding (modular components or single units) or built in. You can rearrange and reconfigure freestanding furniture as needed. Furniture such as an armoire is not only affordable but equally at home in the bedroom, bathroom, and living room. Built-ins provide greater stability and maximize storage potential because they are tailored precisely to your space and possessions.

Decisions such as whether to use open or closed shelves depend on the items you store. Open storage allows you to display and retrieve things easily; closed storage protects possessions and keeps them hidden. Adding drawers or shelves that roll out, slide out, or lift up aids access in cabinets.

STORAGE PLUS STYLE

Storage furniture should be more than functional—it must look good in the room. Whether you choose retail or custom units, consider how the design of the storage unit will fit into your decor. Wood tones are traditional, but a piece painted white adds casual elegance to a traditionally decorated room. Shiny black and bright colors lend a fresh, contemporary look.

MULTIPURPOSE FURNITURE

Pieces such as beds with built-in drawers, benches and ottomans with lift-up seats (below), trunk-style coffee tables, and other double-duty furniture can match decor and conceal clutter without taking up living space. Toss a pretty throw over a filing cabinet (below, right) and turn it into an end table in the family room or a nightstand in the bedroom.

quick fixes

Baskets, bins, boxes, tins, and trunks—containers are the keystones of storage. They collect similar items and remove them from view. To get ideas and inspiration, visit specialty stores geared to storage or home-improvement centers offering products for every budget. Or flip through the pages of a catalog filled with a variety of organizers to help you put your house in order.

NEW USES

Look around for potential containers. You may find organizers that can be adapted for other uses, like pretty baskets, wide-mouthed jars, and ornamental cookie tins. A hanging shoe bag, for instance, might hold children's toys, short-handled garden tools, or magazines for a bathroom library. Hatboxes might hold knitting needles and yarn in a family room (below).

VERSATILE ORGANIZERS

It's easy to find appealing containers to match the scale, shape, and style of your room. To determine the type of organizer that will best serve your needs, measure what you plan to store and the space it will occupy. Then find a container with these dimensions that matches the room's decor. The right containers fill available spaces, turning underutilized shelves and furniture into efficient models of storage.

THE THREE Bs

Quite simply stated, baskets, boxes, and bins are the most versatile of all containers. They can store everything from mail and linens to vegetables and firewood. Handsome baskets come in all sizes and shapes: tall for umbrellas, wide for magazines, and lightweight for laundry (top). Boxes, too, run the gamut in size and color, from basic brown cardboard for long-term storage to patterned paper for display. Colorful, easy-to-lift bins capably stack newspapers, sort clothes, and round up everything from bath accessories to toys.

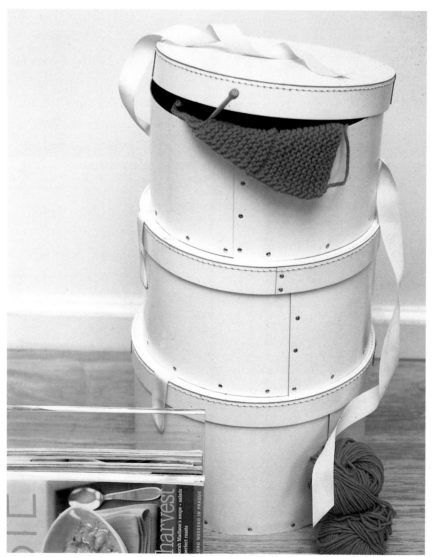

CAPABLE COORDINATES

Rather than mixing styles, consider keeping containers coordinated within rooms. For example, use wicker baskets in living and dining areas, glass bottles or plastic organizers in baths (above), clear glass jars or attractive wood containers in the kitchen, colorful paper boxes in bedrooms, and sturdy plastic or cardboard boxes in the garage.

DIVIDERS Compartments within containers keep contents neat and accessible (above). Adding dividers organizes space inside large containers, making it simple to retrieve items. Partitioning shelves with organizers such as baskets or boxes gives them a unified look. Using dividers in see-through containers keeps contents in view.

STACKABLES Stack containers when possible. Not only does this save floor space, but a stack of creatively arranged organizers adds a whimsical touch to most rooms. Trunks in graduated sizes or a series of sturdy cartons might hide magazines or videos while serving as an end table. A tower of attractive cubes might hold photo albums and flat-file boxes for kids' artwork (left). An ensemble of kitchen tins filled with an assortment of cookies, teas, and spices invites inspection.

room-by-room solutions

E ach space in your home has its own particular purpose—and its own individual storage needs. Different spaces and layouts require that you tackle each room independently and come up with specific solutions tailored to the space and its contents. Every chapter in this book offers creative ideas for storage, from attic to basement and living room to garden shed.

ENTRYWAYS These transition zones should be welcoming areas with space for easy exits and entrances. Organizing a tiny hall might involve wall hangers, small-scale storage furniture (right), or even a hall closet makeover.

GATHERING PLACES The area where your family gets together to talk, entertain, or relax needs maximum storage that matches the room's style. Think horizontal to start, with floor-to-ceiling open shelves or tall cabinets (above). Where space is tight, consider furniture that doubles as storage, window seats with bins or drawers, corner cabinets, and armoires.

BEDROOMS Over the years, bedrooms have become restful refuges for adults and playrooms for children. Maximizing storage by reworking and adding closet space (above), reorganizing drawers, and setting up display space for personal possessions creates the correct environment for those pursuits. Designing storage for kids starts with an expandable system that keeps pace with both their growth and interests.

KITCHENS In the kitchen, you need plenty of easy-access storage; finding space to stow items used daily—or occasionally—is key. Storing kitchen paraphernalia is easier with today's creative new systems and products that expand cabinet and drawer capacity. If you have a closet or even an empty wall, you have space for a pantry (left) or family message center.

Laundry areas and mud-
rooms are utility rooms that collect
everything from muddy boots to
pet bowls and often double as hobby
centers. Shelves and cabinets help
accommodate both functions
(below). For bonus space, search
hallways and even under the stairs.

BATHROOMS Though larger and
better designed now, bathrooms are
still functional spaces. Storage of
grooming aids and personal products
remains much the same—in hangers, shelves, and attractive vanity
cabinets (above). New space savers
include towel ladders, accessory
organizers, and storage furniture.

HOME OFFICES Working at home
requires furniture that blends into
the surroundings and keeps the area
clutter-free. Modular pieces with
matching mobile carts and cabinets,
filing cabinets disguised as furniture,
and wall units tailored to fit the area
(left) help achieve these goals.

**GARAGES, ATTICS, AND BASE-
MENTS** Everything without a
home seems to end up in these
areas, making them prime targets for
reorganization. Ideal for seasonal or
long-term storage, these sites need
systems to keep items used frequently
within reach (right) and items used
occasionally out of sight.

OUTDOOR AND GARDEN Tool
hutches, potting benches, patio
boxes, cupboards (above), and storage sheds are some of the sensible
sites that keep decks and patios
tidy and gardening stress-free.
Garden gear and supplies need to
be organized and stored in dry,
accessible places.

chapter two

entryways

YOUR FRONT ENTRANCE IS A TRANSITION ZONE, an area that allows family and friends to enter and leave your house with maximum pleasure and minimum fuss. Because the entryway offers visitors the first view of your home, its significance is greater than its size. Whether you have a small, cozy entry or a grand, spacious foyer, it should be as efficiently organized as it is warm and welcoming. Stylish furnishings and accessories scaled to fit the front entry space—such as a slim console table, a handy chair, or an attractive mirror—can keep you organized while giving a preview of the decorating style of the rest of your home.

On the following pages you will find dozens of simple ideas for stowing mail, keys, coats, and other items that tend to gravitate toward the front entrance. You will also learn how to retrofit an entry closet to make it more useful and how to take advantage of the often-neglected space in and around the front stairs.

first impressions

Because your entrance hall also functions as your family's traffic route, it's inevitable that purses, jackets, and other day-to-day essentials end up there. Neatly corralling the clutter in a little pocket of space minimizes public view and helps ensure obstacle-free exits and entrances. Fortunately, even a minute front hall has surprising storage capability once you consider all the possibilities.

HOOKS, PEGS, AND OTHER HANG-UPS

Don't overlook the walls of your front hall when floor space is at a premium. Even the smallest entryway has room to add hooks, pegs, and other functional but decorative hang-ups to handle hats, bags, keys, incoming mail, and coats (top and right). Specialty stores, home-improvement centers, and mail-order catalogs present a wealth of practical, good-looking pieces. Or if you're handy, try fashioning your own.

KEY COLLECTORS The trick to locating keys easily is labeling them, placing them in one spot, and never yielding to the temptation to toss them somewhere else. In the entryway, hang keys from hooks fitted inside a wall-hung cupboard (below).

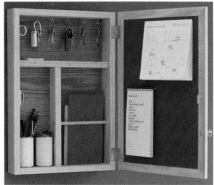

MANAGING MAIL To simplify the collecting and sorting of mail in your entryway, hang attractive containers on the inside doorknob of your front door. Or add a multi-tiered organizer to a wall and make it easy to distribute incoming mail to family members and store outgoing mail (below). Place a pretty basket nearby for tossing unwanted items.

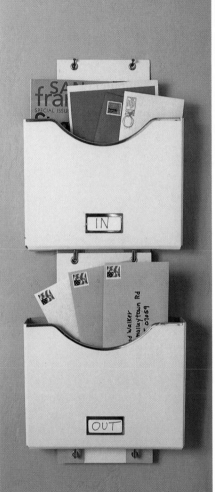

MIRROR IMAGES The entry is a perfect spot for an attractive mirror outfitted with hooks for hats, keys, purses, and umbrellas (above). A properly equipped mirror will expand storage capacity while reflecting light and visually enlarging the entry area. If space or funds prohibit hanging a large wall-mounted mirror, consider placing a smaller one on a shelf or hanging a full-length mirror inside the hall closet door for checking your appearance before you leave the house.

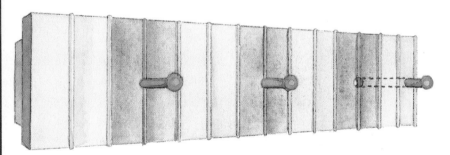

BEADBOARD RACK

Beadboard adds old-fashioned charm to a hang-up. Screw a board of desired length and width into the wall, securing it to studs. Attach a beadboard panel; paint or stain. Insert a row of decorative hooks or drill holes for painted pegs.

shelves and wall units

The size and style of your entrance hall—and your budget—dictate the best type of storage for your possessions. Installing ready-made or ready-to-assemble bracket-mounted and wall-hung shelves is the easiest and least expensive way to provide storage. You can also build your own, with materials, spans, and supports from lumberyards or home-improvement centers.

DECORATIVE LEDGES If space is limited, an attractive basket or tray on a foyer ledge makes an instant storage repository. Adding a lip to the ledge keeps items in place, and painting the ledge the color of your room's trim turns it into an accent piece. For a lasting impression, use your entry as an art gallery. Install two ledges—stacked one above the other—and place taller pieces on the top ledge and shorter pieces on the bottom one (below).

CUBBIES Cubbyholes are organized, easy-to-reach-into spots where family members can pick up or put away belongings as they dash in or out the front door. When selecting cubbies, be sure their size fits your item-specific needs and the width of the entry. Don't forget about depth, which is particularly important when positioning an organizer near the front door. Wall-hung (above) or freestanding, cubbies are widely available at retail stores and come in many styles and finishes. To lend panache to cubbies, paint the insides a rich color that complements your walls.

MULTIPLE AND GRADUATED SHELVES A series of shelves can store large and small items without overwhelming an entry. Use narrow shelves for collectibles and books (below), and deeper shelves for storage organizers, such as attractive baskets and bins. To unify shelves of differing sizes, use brackets with the same profile. Hooks for frequently used keys can be screwed into side brackets.

BUILT-INS Built-in shelves and wall units are particularly well suited to odd-sized spaces. When recessed into existing walls, they save valuable floor space; when built out from existing walls, they provide floor-to-ceiling storage (above). An amply sized foyer can do double duty as a family library or home office when outfitted with built-ins.

shaker style

"FORM FOLLOWS FUNCTION" describes the Shaker philosophy. The 19th-century religious order is widely celebrated for its practical use of space and design. One of the Shakers' most enduring storage ideas was the high pegboard that lined each room of their dwellings. From hats and coats to brooms and mirrors, everything possible was hung up when it was time to clean. Because beds were too big to lift, wooden casters were added to raise them off the floor.

The Shakers' simple, elegant furniture had no veneers, inlays, or decorative carving. Freestanding cabinets and chests were built without feet or base moldings. Many drawers and closed cupboards were part of a wall, becoming the prototype for today's built-in storage.

functional foyer furniture

Your entry can become much more than a pass-through if you take full advantage of all the space, including acquiring furniture that stores with style. With properly scaled pieces, a front entrance is not only an efficient welcoming zone but a storage area for virtually anything if your furniture has concealed compartments. If your house lacks a proper entry, try to carve out a few square feet from a room near the front door, perhaps screening it with one or two ornamental yet hard-working pieces of furniture (right).

TABLES AND CHESTS A small console table with a pull-out drawer or two provides a convenient surface for a key depository, a mail sorter, and a notepad for messages. Use the often-wasted space underneath the table for stacking vintage suitcases (left) or placing a pair of small ottomans side by side.

Another option is a shallow, slim chest with a series of drawers or shelves. Even a sturdy low chest can double as a seat and storage piece. Top it with a decorative bowl, and it becomes a one-stop drop for mail.

STAND-INS Fortunately, those versatile Victorian space savers—hat racks, umbrella stands, and hall trees (below)—have regained favor in modern homes. Using minimal floor space, these functional vertical pieces come in a variety of styles and sizes. Be creative in their use: A vintage hat rack, for example, could also hold purses, shopping bags, or lightweight backpacks.

SEATING SPACE Every entry needs a convenient spot close to the front door for people to sit for a moment, lay down a package or purse, and pull off or put on shoes. Among the choices are a bench with storage inside (above) and a comfy chair with storage containers below. If you have space, a second chair can be used to hold magazines, books, or a plant until the chair is needed for extra seating.

DOUBLE-DUTY ACCESSORIES
Sturdy baskets, boxes, and trunks with flat lids are other good stand-ins, serving as both furniture and storage units. Use them singly as seats or tables; pile them up to minimize floor space and maximize their display potential. You can match baskets to the room's decor by painting their exterior the color of the walls, keeping the interior natural for best wear. Place baskets or attractive bins in an entry to separate newspapers, packages, and magazines, or to collect unwanted items for recycling (right).

Common wall closets are typically 36 to 40 inches wide and 22 to 24 inches deep. These poorly illuminated, spartan spaces usually have one shelf 16 to 20 inches deep above a single rod for hangers. By dividing the space vertically and horizontally to suit your needs and installing the correct storage system, you can gain valuable room for what you need to store. Clear out the closet and take a look inside to get an idea of its potential.

Decide what you want to store, how much room each item requires, and the best way to store it. Figure out how much space you need to allot for hanging items (including guest coats), and how many shelves, storage boxes, cubbies, and over-the-door hooks or racks you will need. When the closet is bare, it's the ideal time to paint the inside and add lighting.

Installing wooden partitions and shelving is an inexpensive way to divide and conquer your space. However, building, finishing, and painting them takes time. Many ready-to-assemble closet systems are available at home-improvement centers and specialty storage stores. But the kits will cost more than lumber and might not be a perfect fit for your space. A combination approach may work better: build partitions and simple shelves and then fit retail units into the home-made skeleton. Off-the-shelf units can be cut to fit your space.

Retail systems are made in two basic styles: wood or melamine units and plastic-coated wire grids. Before purchasing, take careful measurements of your closet, plan the space for the items you need to store, and then sketch your ideal solution on graph paper. Take that with you to the store to select the right units and the hardware to install them. Some stores will completely plan and install a closet system; others cater to do-it-yourselfers.

Some hanging space is necessary for any entry closet. But if you also use this closet to store a host of other items, limit hanging space to hold only your in-season coats and those of visitors. Try to keep the floor space clear, except for a pair of mules or clogs that you slip on for trips outside to fetch the morning paper.

DOOR SPACE The space on the inside of the entry-closet door often goes unused. An over-the-door rack holds pet leashes, a purse, an exercise mat, a yoga bag, a hat, an umbrella, gloves, and other items you might pick up on your way out (A).

CONTAINERS ON SHELVES Ironing supplies are concealed in a basket on one shelf; other baskets hide cameras, binoculars, maps, and scarves (B). If you want to view stored items, select see-through containers.

USE THE SPACE UP HIGH Reserve the hard-to-reach space at the top of a closet for overnight bags, larger suitcases, or anything else you use infrequently (B).

CUBBIES AND HOOKS The vacuum cleaner and ironing board are contained in a single large cubby. A frequently used hand vacuum is conveniently mounted on a wall hook for easy retrieval. When cool, the iron rests on a wall-mounted rack (C).

A

B

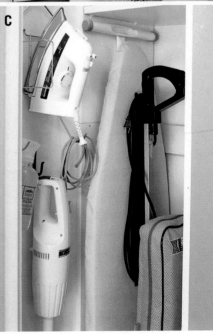

C

steps to storage

When space is tight, an entry stairway can become one of a home's most useful features, offering many possibilities for storage and display. Hiding in plain view, the wedge of space beneath the staircase usually has room to fit a storage cabinet or file drawer between the vertical supports for the treads. But with a little creative design, you may discover that the staircase offers enough space for a closet, small home office, or library.

STAIR BASICS

Enclosed stairs are not difficult to open up because their structural support is not in the wall but in the stringer—the angled piece that joins the treads and risers. The stringer gets support from two floors, so cutting away the wall and studs will not impair stair stability. Before you begin any construction project, check with a state-licensed contractor who knows the local building codes and can advise you on your construction project.

BELOW-STAIRS CLOSETS To take advantage of the space under stairs, you can add storage units that slide out like drawers, making items immediately and fully accessible (above).

The spacious area below treads in a front hall can also be carved out and left open. Install simple, open shelves for shoes, making each pair easy to reach. Add decorative hangers for hats in the space above the shelves. Finish this open closet by adding door casing to match other trim throughout the house (left).

LIBRARY WALL Twelve-inch-deep shelves recessed into a wall that borders a stair run make a perfect place for a library (below). As you go up and down the stairs, you'll be at eye level with the shelves. When you want to stop and browse, simply pick a step and sit down.

WORKING ROOM If you lack a home office, use the space beneath a staircase for a compact one. An understairs area that is 3 feet wide and 4 feet long has enough room for the basics: a desk, computer, and telephone (above). Consult an electrician about adding electrical wiring to provide enough power for your computer equipment and adequate task lighting. Spotlights can be mounted on a track that follows the underside of the stairs. Finish the area with wallboard, a coat of drywall primer, and two coats of your favorite paint. The only potential drawback to your new home office is that you may hear noise from traffic up and down the stairs if they are used frequently. And be cautious about hanging art on the wall—it could loosen due to the vibrations caused by people walking overhead.

THE FRENCH LAUNDRY COOKBOOK · THOMAS KELLER

Colors of Provence

YES NO DESIGN   LOVE

DIANA HER LIFE IN FASHION   GEORGINA HOWELL

LIFE Sixty Years A 60TH ANNIVERSARY CELEBRATION 1936–1996

inside Janne Faulkner

TRIBUTES   CELEBRATING FIFTY YEARS OF NEW YORK CITY BALLET

STOUT   HABANOS   THE STORY OF THE HAVANA CIGAR

chapter three

gathering places

Panasoni

A GATHERING PLACE IS THE HUB OF A HOUSE, the spot where everyone gets together to chat, play games, watch television, listen to music, or simply relax. It may be a living room, family room, recreation room, live-in dining room, or, in today's open shared-space style, a great room.

Finding places to stow and stash the bits and pieces of daily life in a room where so many activities take place can be a challenge. Concocting a storage strategy that puts the nooks and crannies of your space to work can be as simple as adding storage space where an object is used: a drawer for books in a window seat, slide-out racks for CDs in a media cabinet, wall-mounted shelves for collections. From custom cabinetry to freestanding furniture, this chapter presents practical ideas and stylish storage solutions for putting everything in its place.

assessing your space

All gathering places are prone to clutter, but different rooms have different storage needs. Organizing a formal living or dining room may be focused more on display than on hiding things away. Where formal and informal living spaces are combined, however, antiques meet electronics, toys and games jostle photo and art collections, and every square inch of storage must count.

LIVING ROOM

Like the Victorian parlor from which it descended, the separate living room once served as a home's main gathering place. When a more casual family room was added in the early 1960s, the traditional living room became a special space for greeting guests. With the advent of the open plan, it became an oasis for quiet pursuits. Traditional living rooms are typically used for storing books and audio systems, and showcasing artwork or personal possessions.

BOOK NOOK   A bookcase can fit unobtrusively into most living rooms. To increase storage space without detracting from the room's ambience, you might add a bookshelf over the door. A cased opening into the room can be transformed into a mini-library with bookshelves built out from the wall (right).

AUDIO CABINET If a living room contains a sound system, one inconspicuous solution is to place it behind doors in a handsome cabinet (below). Upscale retail cabinets in wood and synthetic materials are widely available. Custom-built media cabinets are tailored to fit stereo components.

SMART FURNITURE Custom built-ins may be a good way to create unobtrusive storage and display space, but it also helps to buy smart furniture. Look for coffee tables (above) and end tables that have drawers or shelves in addition to a pleasing design. Or substitute a small chest for a side table. For functional-plus storage, don't forget that piano benches and footstools conceal valuable storage space beneath their lift-up seats.

showcasing artwork

YOU NO LONGER HAVE TO HAMMER nails in the wall to hang your fine paintings and prized photos. The latest trend in art exhibition is to simply lean artwork against the wall. Pieces are grouped together, often overlapping. Designers believe this creates an informal space, one that lends a bit of irreverence to the pieces.

One way to build your own rotating gallery is to affix a narrow shelf to the wall at the height you would normally hang a picture. Add a front lip or a groove to keep frames in place. You can also display artwork on pegs driven into the wall, using the pegs as a base to support the art.

FAMILY ROOM

A family room hardly needs defining. It's that casual place where every-one "hangs out," and it serves so many purposes that creative storage is a must. Look outside the box for ideas. Adjustable shelving, containers on casters, drawers, and television bays (below) competently organize the paraphernalia that tends to clutter family activity spaces, and they also artfully display prized collectibles.

STACKABLE MODULES If you can't find the modular units to fit your space, think about stackable display cubes. They are sold through retail catalogs, container stores, and home-improvement centers and come in a variety of materials, including galvanized steel (above).

You can make your own from ¾-inch plywood or particleboard in the shapes and sizes that suit your space. Nail or screw boxes together, sand them, and finish with poly-urethane or enamel. Add doors to one or more of the boxes to keep the contents hidden. You can make a simple seat by placing two or more boxes together and adding a cushioned top.

TWO-FOR-ONE FURNISHINGS
Storage furniture has obvious advantages—it's movable and it can be selected to match your decor and needs. For example, a metal frame fitted with baskets that slide out like drawers is an inexpensive way to organize writing supplies, magazines, phone books, and games (below). A flat-topped wicker trunk or a chest with drawers becomes a coffee table or an end table. Collect small items like coasters, playing cards, and reading glasses in a basket or a pretty bowl placed high enough on a shelf that all you see is the container.

shared spaces

MANY MODERN HOMES COMBINE kitchen, dining, living, and entertaining functions in one big room without physical or visual barriers. In this open plan, activity zones and traffic patterns are organized merely by furniture placement and aptly named area rugs.

Storage is paramount in shared spaces, and each space may require a different storage strategy. Functional furniture is invaluable since it provides storage and delineates activity areas. For example, a console table placed behind a sofa to hold collectibles and other objects also acts as a room divider, setting off the seating area from the kitchen. Low bookcases work as space dividers, too, with a combination of open and closed shelves allowing display room on both sides.

Walls of storage are popular in open spaces. With cabinets, drawers, and shelving, storage walls provide places for the items that accumulate in family living spaces, such as magazines, remote controls, and toys. The walls also offer room to stylishly display decorative items.

ROOM TO PLAY Built-in cabinets and modular systems both feature plenty of organized space to stash cards, games, and art supplies. Using baskets, boxes, or trays to hold items for different activities makes it easy to put them away. A roll-around storage bin parks in its own "garage" underneath a cabinet to hide toys (right).

MEDIA ROOM

Most gathering places revolve around the electronic hearth. But planning a space for watching television is more challenging if the room serves other purposes. No matter where you put it or how you try to hide it, a media center becomes the focal point of the room.

Major storage and organizing decisions depend on the sizes and shapes of your audio/visual gear. Increasingly complex entertainment systems—including televisions, VCRs, DVD players, TiVo recorders, and stereo equipment—require substantial, well-planned storage.

TV VIEWS Television screens should be placed where glare won't interfere with daytime viewing and where sight lines are good from anywhere in the room. If a television is concealed in a cabinet or armoire (left), make sure the enclosed space is well ventilated; heat buildup eventually kills transistors and printed circuits. Wide-screen, flat-panel televisions (some as thin as 2 inches) can hang almost anywhere (above). But any television can be removed from the traffic pattern if you put it on a shelf or suspend it from the wall with a special bracket. Adding an attractive container can organize all remotes (below).

ELECTRONIC COMPONENTS

Stack audio and video components in or out of sight, in a custom tower, on a rack, or in furniture adapted for the task. Position components at a height that makes it easy to read their controls (facing page; top).

VIDEOS, DVDs, AND CDs

Versatile storage systems for media accessories come in a variety of combinations that can be amended or extended to fit your changing needs. Hanging CD holders, high-tech cabinets with pull-out shelves or drawers (top, far right), and metal or plastic dividers and trays (bottom, far right) that hold tapes and discs upright are options. Small towers look nice and take up minimal floor space, but choose one without individual, preset slots so that you don't have to shuffle the entire collection to find space for a new piece (right).

standard sizes of media accessories

KNOWING THE SIZES AND SHAPES OF THE MEDIA ACCESSORIES you own ensures that the items fit the allotted space. Measure the items you want to organize before building or purchasing a storage unit.

DVD — $7\frac{1}{2}$" × $5\frac{3}{8}$"

LP or laser disc — $12\frac{3}{8}$" × $12\frac{3}{8}$"

Videotape — $7\frac{1}{2}$" × $4\frac{1}{8}$"

CD — 5" × $5\frac{5}{8}$"

Audiocassette — $4\frac{1}{4}$" × $2\frac{3}{4}$"

DINING ROOM

More than any other room in the house, the dining room has fallen victim to lifestyle changes. Few home owners have space to spare, and what was once a room reserved for family suppers and formal dinners now doubles as a library, sewing studio, or homework headquarters. When the dining area has fuzzier boundaries—a space in a breakfast nook or a table off the kitchen—efficient space planning and storage help to fully utilize it.

FURNITURE FINDS   Mixing good-looking storage pieces with built-in cabinets and shelves creates interest. If pieces are the same scale, don't worry about using several styles in one room. You can find breakfronts (top, left), sideboards, china cabi-nets, and buffets (left) in many styles and prices. Any of these dining room pieces make elegant display cases while providing extra shelving.

If you have room for a built-in, a good choice is a wall unit with glass doors and lighted shelves to display china (facing page; top, right). Drawers below hold additional place settings, glasses, and linens.

NOOKS AND CRANNIES   A nook can incorporate a freestanding china cabinet. Or an alcove can be filled with a cabinet, shelves, and a wine rack. Even space between the wall studs can be turned into shelves for serving and silver pieces. Or build a shallow cabinet with recycled doors for colorful glassware (right).

Compact cupboards tucked in a corner of the room add display space. Corner hutches eat up very little floor space, yet a pair can stow almost as much as a breakfront. For a built-in look, buy unfinished versions and paint them to match the trim in your room.

DISH DISPLAY   Take advantage of every space to showcase treasures. Install a plate rail on one wall (right), cluster a pottery collection or serving pieces atop a cabinet, or stack china in a compact wrought-iron étagère (left).

DOUBLE-DUTY DINING Take a new look at your dining room and think about updating the space for another purpose. Floor-to-ceiling cabinets or shelves can provide space to store books, flatware, candlesticks, and little-used serving pieces. Neatly arrange piles of your favorite art books, and top each one with a ceramic bowl or teapot to retain the dining-room ambience (right). Or turn space in a small home with a less formal dining area into a place to store games, puzzles, art supplies, and seasonal decorations.

If you have a large book collection, line a wall in your dining room with a series of bookcases that will house your family library (above). Add a comfortable chair and good lighting, and the dining room becomes a quiet place to peruse a classic, thumb through a garden journal, or tackle nightly homework after the dishes have been cleared.

STACKABLE STORAGE
Storage modules that can be piled on top of each other offer even more flexibility than stock cabinets. Concoct an artful array of cubbies and tie them together with a serving ledge or decorative cornice.

storing linens and tableware

EVERYDAY DISHES, GLASSES, cutlery, and tablecloths get a lot of use—and abuse; the tableware saved for special occasions needs better protection. Even though it may be used for formal outings only, tableware still should be kept within easy reach because the more difficult it is to get to, the less likely you are to use it.

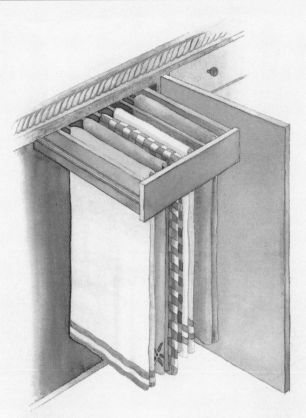

■ Hang tablecloths, place mats, and napkins from large wooden dowels in a cabinet outfitted with a bottomless drawer (right). Linens stay neatly ironed and are well displayed for quick selection.

■ To keep flatware free from scratches and tarnish, store pieces in special silverware boxes or in divided drawers or trays lined with soft anti-tarnish fabric.

■ Crystal can be packed away in pouches, although most people prefer to display it in cases. Adding glass doors to cabinets helps keep pieces dust-free and protected from breakage.

■ Zippered padded pouches with built-in separators are a favorite way to store china. To find pieces easily, attach labels. If you stack your plates on a shelf, use separators between them to keep them scratch-free. You can buy separators at kitchen, linen, and container stores or make them from a soft fabric, such as felt.

PROJECT: dining-room cupboard

Don't underestimate the magic of tasteful trim, such as the dentil crown molding used to dress up this cupboard. You can make your own cupboard, but it's easy to buy an unfinished bookcase and modify it. Cabinet doors with arched tops or glass inserts can be ordered from local cabinetmakers and home-improvement centers. Simply attach them with European-style hinges and add stylish knobs.

MATERIALS

- One piece of 4-by-8-ft. ³⁄₄-in. maple plywood
- One piece of 4-by-8-ft. ¹⁄₄-in. maple plywood
- 1-in. and 1¹⁄₂-in. finishing nails
- One 4-ft. length of 1-by-3 lumber
- Four snap-closing, 125-degree hinges
- Two solid-panel doors, 18 by 32¹⁄₂ in.
- Two glass-panel doors, 18 by 31 in. (arch top optional)
- One roll of veneer edging
- 3-by-80 in. primed crown molding
- One tube of white caulk or wood filler
- Three to four decorative knobs or pulls

CUTTING THE PLYWOOD Begin by cutting the ³⁄₄-inch plywood for the sides, shelves, top, and top and kick plates of the cupboard to the following sizes: two pieces at 14 by 84 inches for the sides; seven pieces at 14 by 35 inches for the top and shelves; and two pieces at 3¹⁄₂ by 36 inches for the top and kick plate. Cut the ¹⁄₄-inch plywood to 36 inches wide for the back. See page 184 for instructions on how to make a simple bookcase.

CUTTING DADOES IN THE SIDES Starting at the bottoms of the two 14-by-84-inch boards, make marks at 4, 18, 36, 50, 60, and 72 inches from the ends. With a combination square or right (90-degree) triangle, draw a line at each mark across the face of the boards at a right angle to the 84-inch side. Using a router with a ³⁄₈-inch-diameter bit, set to cut to a ³⁄₈-inch depth, cut grooves across the boards at the marks you have drawn so that the top of each groove aligns with the lines drawn. At the top of both pieces, cut a rabbet joint to accept one of the 14-by-35-inch boards.

RABBETING THE SHELVES Using a router or table saw, cut ³⁄₈-by-³⁄₈-inch rabbet joints in the ends of six of the 14-by-35-inch boards **(A)**. For information on basic joinery and cutting dadoes and rabbets, see pages 182–185.

ASSEMBLING THE CASE Mark lines across the outside faces of both 84-inch boards, ¾ inch lower than the first set of marks for the dadoes. Use these to guide the locations of the nails securing the shelves. Glue and then nail the six rabbeted shelves in place using 1½-inch finishing nails, being careful to align the front edges. Attach the one shelf that is not rabbeted to the top.

Turn the cabinet on its face and nail the back piece of ¼-inch plywood in place with 1-inch finishing nails. Once the back is in place, turn the case right side up and nail the top and kick plates in place. Next, install the hinges on the doors you have made or purchased; adjust as required to keep the doors level.

APPLYING THE VENEER EDGING Cut six pieces of edging about 36 inches long. Heat up a household iron set to "cotton," and iron the edging in place across the face of each shelf. Carefully cut the ends at the point where the shelf meets the side. Apply the edging down both sides, and trim the overlap with a utility knife or razor blade. Turn to page 186 for information on edging.

INSTALLING THE CROWN From the length of 1-by-3 lumber, cut out 13 isosceles triangles in which the two short sides that meet at a right angle are 2 inches; you will attach the crown molding to the

long, diagonal side of these once you have nailed them in place. Nail seven triangles across the front of the cabinet and three across each of the sides, placing them flush with the top of the cabinet so that they don't protrude higher than the top.

Using a miter box or chop saw, measure and cut a 36-inch piece of molding—positioned upside down on the miter box or chop saw—to fit at a 45-degree angle on both sides at the front of the cabinet **(B)**. Nail it in place, attaching it to the long, diagonal sides of the triangle pieces. Measure and cut two more pieces of molding for the sides of the cabinet, making a cut on one side at a 45-degree angle so that it will meet the front piece; cut the other ends of both pieces of molding at a 90-degree angle, so that the ends will meet the wall. Nail the side pieces to the cabinet, taking care that the two 45-degree angles of the front piece match up to the side pieces **(C)**. You can fill the seam with caulk or wood filler if your pieces don't match up perfectly.

FINISHING THE CUPBOARD Set nails below the surface, fill holes with wood filler, and sand with 120-grit sandpaper. Apply a coat of stain and finish, or primer and paint, as desired. See page 187 for more information on setting nails, sanding, and painting. Once the finish is dry, add the decorative knobs or pulls to the cabinet doors.

space savers

When you can't stack stereo gear any higher or wedge one more book into your shelves, it's time to think about adding storage space. Every room has potential unused space; you just need to find the spot—and the perfect storage system. The floor-to-ceiling storage walls, versatile shelving, and furniture shown on the following pages are good places to start.

STORAGE WALLS

People are often loath to give up precious floor space for a wall of storage, yet the result is a more functional and beautiful area. Storage walls range from banks of fixed custom shelves (below) to expansive systems with adjustable shelves, open and closed cabinets, and stacks of drawers. Choices include built-in units, modular components, and manufactured cabinets.

BUILT-INS Use built-ins to tie storage seamlessly into your architectural style or to save space in storage-skimpy rooms. They are well suited to odd-sized spaces where storage furniture can't fit: recessed into a wall, under a staircase, around a window, or over a door (right). You can't take built-ins with you when you move, but they will add value to your home.

MANUFACTURED CABINETS Cabinets like those used in kitchens and bathrooms are another storage option (facing page; top). You can find relatively inexpensive stock models at home-improvement centers and high-end custom creations from a cabinetmaker. As a rule, the semicustom (upgraded stock cabinets available with standard modifications) and custom cabinets are made from higher grade materials, look better, and cost more.

MODULAR SYSTEMS Versatile and easy to install, modular systems come in a staggering diversity of components and myriad types, styles, and designs. Some lean against or fasten to the wall, eliminating the need for shelf backs or other supports (above). Systems arrive preassembled—you mount components on supports— or ready to assemble. As needs change, manufactured systems can be reconfigured: Shelves can be raised or lowered, drawers refitted, and cabinets moved from one location to another.

SHELF CONTROL

Of all storage components, shelves are the most versatile; they don't take up space as much as create it. And open shelves are more accessible and economical than closed cabinets. Shelves can be fixed or adjustable, pull-out, swivel, or lift-up. They can be installed in cabinets, mounted on walls with brackets or other supports, or added to modular systems. Designers suggest dividing long expanses of shelves into thirds, where space permits, for a more visually pleasing placement. For added interest, vary shelf heights.

WALL-MOUNTED SHELVES Glass, wood, or metal—wall-mounted shelves are good choices for organized living spaces. These shelves showcase possessions and add architectural interest to the space. They fit neatly into empty nooks, hang high above furniture, and display collections, photographs, and art to act as a focal point in the room (above).

MOVABLE SHELVES Adding casters to a shelving unit offers you placement flexibility if you regularly change the configuration of your furniture. Dress up mobile units with stock molding and decorative trim. For more visual interest, insert a fabric-covered foam-core board, cut to fit the height and width of the inside back of the shelving unit (left). It's easy to change the unit's spot— and decorating scheme—according to the season or your evolving taste.

BOOKCASES ON THEIR OWN A wealth of shapes, sizes, and styles make freestanding bookcases easy to situate. They increase the storage space in your room without detracting from its decor.

Bookshelves should fit the books you collect. A generous shelf (no deeper than 15 inches) will store most books and electronic gear with ease. Paperbacks need 8- to 10-inch-high shelves. Put larger volumes, such as art books, on lower shelves; use upper shelves for standard sizes (left).

If there's a logical way to return books to a shelf, they are less likely to be left out. Organize books by category: novels and nonfiction, the latter grouped by subject. Some keep libraries intact in one room; others place books where they are read—cookbooks in a kitchen, for example.

standard sizes of books

BOOKS COME IN A VARIETY OF SIZES AND SHAPES, so take an inventory of your library and organize your books by size before you construct or buy a new bookcase.

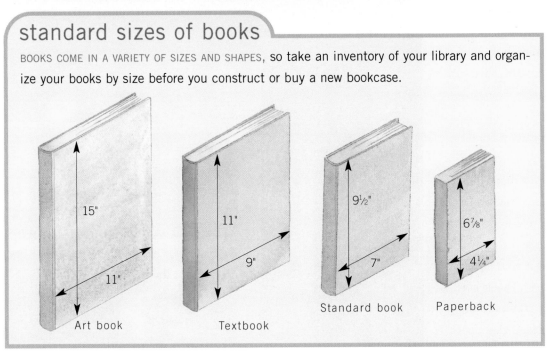

Art book — 15" × 11"
Textbook — 11" × 9"
Standard book — 9½" × 7"
Paperback — 6⅞" × 4¼"

COLLECTION AND DISPLAY SPACE

What you choose to collect in life, whether cartoon lunch boxes, model cars, or art glass, reveals much about you. Because collections have such a personal significance, it's important to display them in ways that enhance their beauty or meaning. For maximum impact, don't scatter your collectibles around a room. Instead, cluster collections on shelves (right).

Draw attention to works of art, such as pottery or photography, by silhouetting them against a plain background (above). Fragile collectibles might be positioned on lighted shelves behind glass doors. Add latches if you live in earthquake country.

CLASSY CONTAINERS Whether you browse the Internet, look at a storage catalog, or walk into a store, chances are you'll be amazed at the variety and good looks of today's organizers. They come in all sizes and shapes. Pick containers the shape and size of the items you want to store, and match them to suit your room's decor.

Filling shelves with attractive baskets or boxes is just one way to coordinate a room and make a space more efficient (right). Use them to organize videotapes and discs, store photographs, or conceal a host of miscellaneous items.

preserving photos

WITH A LITTLE CARE, YOU CAN ENJOY your photos for a long time.
Though photographic films and papers are now more stable and long-lasting, images can still fade or discolor if exposed to excessive light, heat, or moisture. Photos are best stored in a space with a constant temperature below 75 degrees, ruling out most attics and garages.

Plastic sheets, used in most photo albums, can accelerate print deterioration. It's better to keep prints in photo boxes with lids or in flat-file drawers. Separate prints with pieces of acid-free paper or enclose them in individual rag-paper envelopes. Place a packet of silica gel in the container to help absorb moisture.

Protect color slides by storing them in boxed projector trays, file boxes, or special plastic sheets (right). Negatives and slides in protective file sheets can be organized in three-ring binders before placing them on a shelf or in a drawer or box.

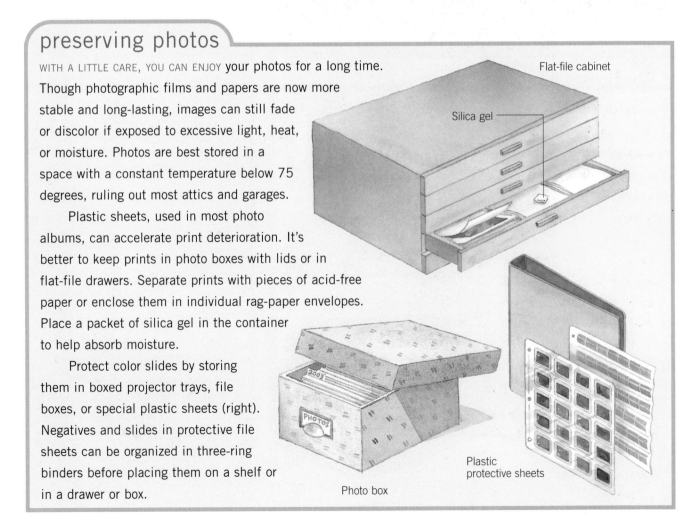

Flat-file cabinet

Silica gel

Photo box

Plastic protective sheets

best storage furniture

When it's time to purchase furniture, your best storage options will be versatile pieces with added drawers, shelves, or bases for tucking away clutter. Visit flea markets and thrift shops for "secondhand antiques" you can refinish or restore. If your budget doesn't allow for a built-in window seat with pull-out drawers, for example, place a sturdy bench or flat-topped trunk underneath the window, adding a cushion for comfort and baskets or trunks below the bench for added storage. Some workhorses of the storage world are highlighted in the next few pages.

ARMOIRES Having migrated from the bedroom, armoires are now employed as handsome, utilitarian storage spots for gathering places. These popular pieces hold anything, from books to bar gear, and offer maximum storage in minimal floor space (below). Pick a style that matches your decorating scheme.

APOTHECARY CHESTS Valuable for its many drawers, an apothecary chest is most useful for the organization of small items. When a chest is placed prominently in a room, its tidy appearance provides star quality that belies its usefulness (right).

SIDEBOARDS Sideboards and buffets are dining room classics. Ideal for serving food and beverages at mealtime, they also provide space to store silver, linens, serving pieces, wine, and more (below). Use them also as display surfaces for pretty pottery, china, or silver. They can be modified to hold files, sewing supplies, and other useful items.

TRUNKS Flat-topped trunks work well as coffee tables (above) or end tables, or even as extra seating. When outfitted inside with trays and baskets, they organize and contain photos, games, magazines, and newspapers.

COFFEE TABLES Coffee tables placed in front of sofas provide convenient spaces to rest books and magazines, drinks and snacks; drawers and baskets hide coasters, cards, and games (left). Canvas pockets around a small coffee table offer stand-up places to hold current magazines (below).

OTTOMANS You can convert an ottoman to a coffee table by placing a large wicker tray on top. Choose an ottoman that is an inch or two lower than the sofa, and add casters for easy movement. Some ottomans open for extra storage (left); one kind conceals a single bed.

TANSUS Japanese wooden storage chests and cabinets, called *tansus*, adapt to almost any room. Available in a variety of sizes and shapes, tansus sometimes have interesting stepped shelves. Both antique and reproduction pieces blend effectively with contemporary and traditional designs. If you're buying one to hold a television and sound system, make sure the appliances fit comfortably inside with enough space for components (right).

CONSOLE AND END TABLES
Equipped with drawers and shelves, console and end tables are invaluable in gathering spaces. The slim profile of the console table enables it to be used almost anywhere storage is needed—behind a couch, in front of a window, or against a wall (left). And end tables do more than just hold lamps—they offer extra surfaces for glasses, books, and special pieces of art (above).

chapter four

kitchens

ALL KITCHENS—BIG OR SMALL, HIGH STYLE OR NO STYLE—will function efficiently if they are well organized. All you have to do is keep your countertops free of clutter and your kitchen paraphernalia in a logical place where anyone can find it quickly and easily. Sound impossible? Not if you have the right storage solutions for your space.

Whether you're renovating your kitchen or working with what you have, start with good planning. It's definitely easier to reorganize your kitchen during a remodel, but you don't have to invest in new cabinetry to improve your storage capacity. From rattan baskets and shelf maximizers to corner lazy Susans and movable islands, there are many products that can transform your kitchen from one you dread entering into one you don't want to leave.

kitchen primer

Before you begin investigating your options, evaluate your storage needs. Start by opening every drawer and cabinet, and take inventory of your kitchen contents. Are you able to store things near where they are used? Can you find each item without having to move several others aside? And most important, can you get rid of seldom-used kitchenware that takes up valuable space?

SORTING THINGS OUT

Ideally, you want to store items you use regularly in proximity to the kitchen's five main work areas: refrigerator, stove, food preparation, sink/cleanup, and serving. If your kitchen is large enough, you may have the space for a menu-planning/office area as well. By storing things where you use them, you can cook and clean up more quickly and efficiently than before.

THE WORK TRIANGLE In an efficient kitchen plan, the three most heavily used work areas—the refrigerator, sink, and cook-top—should be laid out so that the lines between them form a triangle in which no single leg is shorter than 4 feet or longer than 9 feet. Generally, the counter space within or adjacent to this triangle is used for food preparation. Since this is the busiest area of the kitchen, all of your frequently used items, from utensils and culinary equipment to cooking products, should be stored in the area of first use. Anything that isn't used for preparation or cooking can be stored outside of the work triangle.

Once you know where you want to locate each item within the kitchen, consider how it will be stored. Most items can be sorted into one or more of four functional categories: access easily, display, keep out of sight, or organize. The following pages of this chapter present ideas about how and where to store your kitchen items once you've done the initial work of sorting them into one of these four categories.

TYPICAL WORK TRIANGLES

The most efficient work triangles are found in U-shaped, L-shaped, and galley kitchen designs, as illustrated here. Identify your work triangle, and store the food preparation and cooking items you use regularly inside it.

L-SHAPED
This work triangle allows for plenty of counter work space. If there is sufficient room for it, an island will increase your overall undercounter storage area.

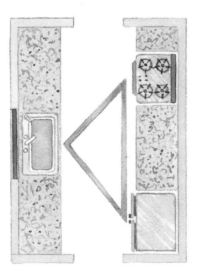

GALLEY STYLE
This narrow, corridor-style layout makes the best use of a small space. Upper cabinets should cover both walls to maximize storage.

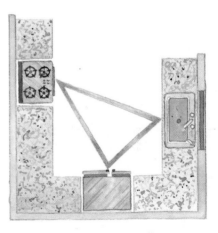

U-SHAPED
When you have enough distance between opposite walls, a U-shaped arrangement provides maximum upper and base cabinet storage, as well as considerable counter space.

easy access

You use some of the items you store in your kitchen daily, and others—such as the chafing dish you inherited from your great-aunt Martha—make a brief appearance on special occasions. Once you've sorted out the items you use constantly, you'll want to store them in their proper work areas. When it's easy to find everything, several people can work together without getting in each other's way.

Given the number of ways to maximize kitchen storage, you shouldn't feel limited by the size or shape of your kitchen. Consider these ideas for rearranging your storage areas so you can keep everything you use right where you need it.

POTS AND PANS Have them at the ready, nestled in drawers in a base cabinet (below) or hanging from a rack (right). Deep drawers and pull-out shelves are perfect for stockpots. Shallower drawers work well for frying pans and woks.

Store cookie sheets, broiler pans, and cutting boards vertically in a narrow cabinet near the oven (facing page; top). There they are easier to remove and put away than when piled on a shelf. Shallow sliding shelves made of wood or oversize baking pans are ideal for tart pans, cake forms, cookie molds, and other specialty baking items (right).

UTENSILS Locate spoons, spatulas, whisks, and ladles as close to the stove and food-preparation area as possible. A wide-mouthed ceramic jar (below) or shallow drawers provide ample space for most cooking utensils. When countertop or drawer space is limited, hang utensils from a metal rod or rack mounted to the backsplash or an adjacent wall (below, right).

KNIVES Separate knives and keep them next to the cutting surface. Slots in a cutting board (right), a magnetic wall strip, or a freestanding block (bottom, left) will keep blades safe. When storing knives in a drawer (below), use knife inserts to keep blades from rubbing against each other and becoming dull.

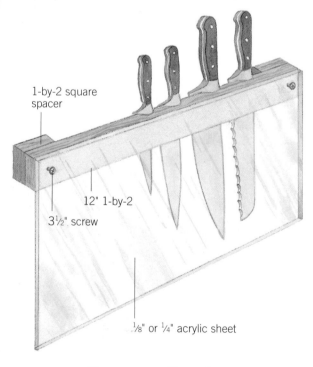

1-by-2 square spacer

12" 1-by-2

3½" screw

⅛" or ¼" acrylic sheet

TRANSPARENT KNIFE RACK

This wall rack can be assembled using 1-by-2 lumber and a ⅛- or ¼-inch sheet of clear acrylic. The acrylic sheet should be at least ½ inch longer than the blade of your longest knife.

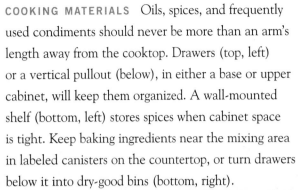

COOKING MATERIALS Oils, spices, and frequently used condiments should never be more than an arm's length away from the cooktop. Drawers (top, left) or a vertical pullout (below), in either a base or upper cabinet, will keep them organized. A wall-mounted shelf (bottom, left) stores spices when cabinet space is tight. Keep baking ingredients near the mixing area in labeled canisters on the countertop, or turn drawers below it into dry-good bins (bottom, right).

to the inside of the cabinet door. A sink-front tilt-out drawer (left) provides a resting place for vagabond sponges and scrub brushes. Consider hanging your dish drainer and paper towels from a metal-rod wall system next to the sink instead of having them take up valuable counter or undercounter space.

CLEANING SUPPLIES Use the space under your sink to store cleaning materials and garbage if you don't have room for a designated pull-out bin within your base cabinetry. There are many configurations of pull-out baskets (right), towel racks, and bins designed specifically for this space, as well as those that attach

wheelchair access

ACCESSIBILITY IS NOT just a convenience but a necessity if you are in a wheelchair. When planning your kitchen, everything you use regularly should be comfortably within your seated reach.

Ideally, the space below the sink and cooktop should be left open to accommodate your wheelchair. The dishwasher can be elevated so you don't have to bend over when you insert and remove dishes. The microwave should be no higher than the countertop.

Most items should be stored 15 to 48 inches from the floor on the countertop or in pull-out vertical pantries, shelves, and drawers. You can outfit the backsplash behind a wheelchair-accessible countertop with a metal rod and hang utensils, pots, and pans from it. While most overhead storage is off-limits to anyone in a wheelchair, pull-down shelves available from specialty manufacturers can be mounted in upper cabinets, enabling you to take advantage of once-unreachable storage.

DISHWARE Dishes are easiest to handle if they are stored near where they are cleaned. Stack them in a cabinet by the sink or dishwasher between waist and chest height so that they are easy to put away and lift out. Plates you use every day are easy to reach in a plate rack on the countertop (top, right) or in a deep drawer with vertical dividers (right). Air-dry and store special china and crystal in a cabinet retrofitted with stainless steel racks, a bottom pan underneath to catch water drops, and its own drain (above).

on display

As the kitchen has become a central meeting place for family and friends, presentation has become a priority for many home owners. It is now fashionable to display almost everything in the kitchen—from dishes to pots and pans to gourmet oils and vinegars. Cabinetmakers and storage manufacturers have risen to the occasion with attractive display cases, baskets, canisters, and racks.

THE PROS AND CONS

The most obvious benefit of keeping your wares out in the open is that they are easy to reach. A tasteful display can add character to a kitchen. But before you unhinge your cabinet doors and install open shelving, consider what you have to display and what kind of housekeeper you are. You should be prepared to keep these displays in perfect order—if items are thrown randomly onto shelves and into baskets, your kitchen will have a sense of chaos.

Additionally, displayed items require frequent cleaning. Kitchen paraphernalia on open shelves or in baskets collects dust. Unless you regularly use and wash items, such as your everyday dishes and glassware, you may want to keep them behind closed doors.

OPEN SHELVING The most straightforward way to show off your collections is with open shelving. Shelves can be built inside a cabinet box, float on the wall (right), or be suspended by cables. They can be white, stained wood, or brightly colored to complement

what they are holding (above), or they can be made from wire or galvanized metal. Open shelves can be above or under the counter, and you can even string them across a fixed window as a place to hold fresh herbs. You can also buy stand-alone units of open shelving in wood or metal.

GLASS DOORS Use cabinets with glass doors on one or both sides (top, right) to display items you want seen but protected from dust and grease. If you like the sense of openness a glass cabinet provides but not the work required to keep its contents in order, you can choose from a wide range of translucent glasses that obscure what's on the other side (right).

ON THE RACK Consider racks that hang on the wall or under your wall cabinets for holding and displaying a collection of mugs and teacups (below), gourmet oils and vinegars, and even stemware (bottom). Or you can hang a rack from the ceiling to display a favorite set of pots and pans (right).

BASKETS Constructed from rattan or wire, baskets are used to show off produce and sundries in more informal kitchens (above). They can rest on open shelves above or below the countertop (right). To display a collection of baskets, hang them decoratively from the ceiling.

art of arrangement

WHETHER YOU HAVE a special collection you want to showcase or open shelves to fill, you can create an attractive display by following a simple rule: Group items together that share a common characteristic such as type or color—or a combination of the two.

Any group of objects will look agreeable together if they have a similar or complementary shape or color. The simplest displays gather identical items, such as a line of plates or bowls. A display becomes more complex when you group a set of dishware of identical or complementary colors on the same shelf.

If you have a collection of similar items with different shapes, such as teapots or vases, arrange them according to height or width. Condiments in bottles and spices in jars make nice displays if grouped so that their shapes and labels complement each other.

Once you have arranged basic groupings, enhance them by throwing in a visual surprise. A glass pitcher can add interest to a display of colored dishes. Silver mugs complement a group of heavy ceramic bowls.

In the end, your eye is the best judge of what is most appealing. Expect to move things around before you find the arrangement that best represents your style and adds the most character to your kitchen.

PROJECT: hanging pot rack

Although you can purchase a hanging pot rack in many stock sizes, you can also save a little money and add custom touches by constructing one of your own. Build this hanging pot rack with a simple wooden frame, and embellish it with crown molding or wooden fretwork purchased at a home-improvement center. Depending on your skill level, you can rout the edges of the frame for added detail.

MATERIALS

- One 8-ft. piece of 1-by-4 clear Douglas fir board
- Two 3-ft. pieces of 1-in.-diameter wooden dowel
- 1½-in. finishing nails
- Two pieces of wooden fretwork
- Carpenter's glue
- Blue masking tape
- Four eye hooks
- Four J-hooks
- Four toggle bolts (optional, if J-hooks are screwed into ceiling joists)
- Four lengths of metal chain, each 15–20 in. long
- Eight metal S-hooks

CUTTING THE WOOD FOR THE FRAME From the Douglas fir board, cut two 30-inch boards for the sides of the frame and two 16½-inch boards for the ends. Rout the side edges of the four boards for detail, if desired (see page 187 for information on routing an edge). Carefully line up the 30-inch boards next to each other, and draw a line with a pencil across the faces of the boards in the center at 15 inches. Next, draw lines across the faces of both boards at 7 inches from each end (A). You should now have three marks on each board. Using a 1-inch spade bit, drill a ½-inch-deep hole in the center point of each mark, making sure that the holes on both boards line up perfectly.

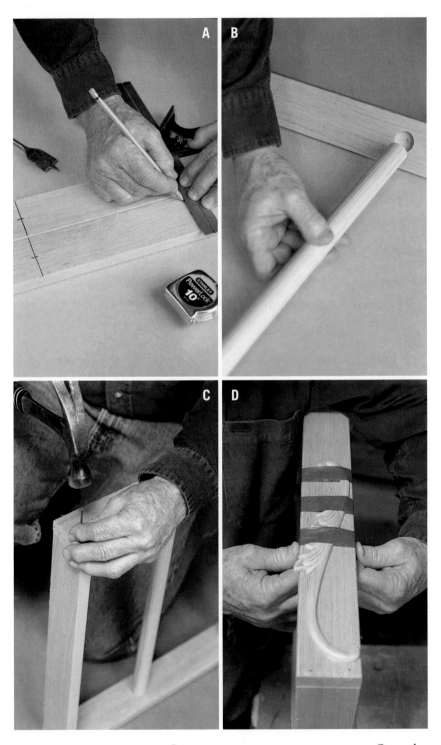

attractive pattern. Secure the glued fretwork with strips of blue masking tape and let the glue dry for at least an hour before removing the tape (**D**).

STAINING OR PAINTING THE RACK

Set all nails below the surface, fill any holes with wood filler, and sand with 120-grit sandpaper. To protect the wood from damage, add a protective finish to the rack. See page 187 for information on paints and finishes.

ATTACHING THE HARDWARE

Screw the eye hooks into the top four corners of the frame. Locate the point on the ceiling where you want to hang the rack. Measure the distance between each of the eye hooks on the rack and mark these measurements on your ceiling, placing them at ceiling joists for the best support. Drill ceiling holes and screw in J-hooks; if you are not nailing into joists, be sure to use toggle bolts to hold the J-hooks in the ceiling. Attach the chains to each eye hook on the rack, and then hang the other ends of the chains from the J-hooks attached to the ceiling. Place the S-hooks on the dowels and hang your pots from them.

INSERTING THE DOWELS Cut three dowels 17$\frac{1}{2}$ inches long. Insert the ends of the dowels into the holes of one of the 30-inch-long side boards (**B**); fit the holes of the second board to the dowels.

FINISHING THE FRAME Once the dowels are in place, nail the end boards to the frame with 1$\frac{1}{2}$-inch finishing nails (**C**). With carpenter's glue, attach the fretwork to the outside of the frame in an

behind closed doors

Most people, when remodeling or reorganizing their kitchens, focus on the exterior of their cabinetry: size, shape, and color. But any real increases in storage capacity happen on the inside. The next few pages provide great ideas for transforming simple cabinets into the most efficient storage systems.

CABINET FACTS

If you remodel, you can control the sizes and types of your cabinets. The simplest cabinets come as empty boxes or with shelves. From there you can select any number of configurations, including pull-out shelves, pull-out baskets, drawers, vertical dividers, lazy Susans, appliance garages, wine cubbies, swivel shelves, and built-in bread boxes.

Most cabinet manufacturers work in widths of 3-inch increments. The most popular widths for kitchen cabinetry are 18, 24, and 30 inches, but 6-inch-wide spaces are perfect for a pull-out vertical spice rack or a narrow wine rack.

A 9-inch width gives you enough space for vertical tray dividers or a small pull-out pantry.

When evaluating your options, consider that deep drawers are more convenient for storing pots and pans than pull-out shelves behind doors. Wide, shallow drawers are better for storing table linens than narrow, deep ones. And if you have a corner with a return of at least 25 inches along the second wall, a corner unit—with or without a lazy Susan—will provide more usable storage space than a straight one.

WALL CABINETS

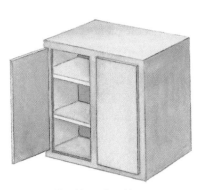
Double wall cabinet

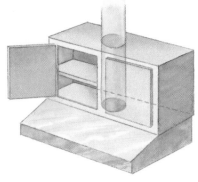
Range cabinet

Fold-out pantry cabinet

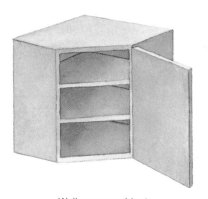
Wall corner cabinet

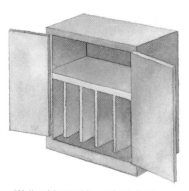
Wall cabinet with vertical dividers

Wall cabinet with appliance garage

Standard base

Three-drawer base

Base with vertical pullout

Double base

Sink base

Base with vertical dividers

Blind corner base with swivel shelves

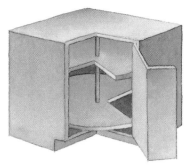

Base with lazy Susan

Base with pull-out shelves

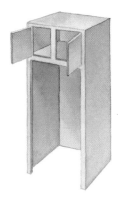

Refrigerator cabinet

Double-door pantry cabinet

Narrow pantry cabinet

CABINET WIZARDRY

The greatest advances in kitchen storage have been made in the storage systems that fit inside cabinets. You can purchase them with new cabinetry or as items you install yourself. Look for these inserts at kitchen and bath dealers, at home-improvement stores and storage-oriented retailers, and through the Internet.

THE PROFICIENT PANTRY Use the pantry for storing nonperishable food and dry goods. You can create a pantry from a dedicated cabinet, a walk-in closet, or freestanding shelving units. The key to a successful pantry is having every item in view. Anything stored at the back of a deep stationary shelf—especially if it is high up or near the floor—risks obsolescence.

If a standard upper, base, or tall cabinet serves as a pantry, you can retrofit it with a vertical pull-out system in wood, plastic, or wire (above). Manufacturers make fold-out inserts for pantries in wood, plastic, or stainless steel. If you use a fold-out insert, you may have enough space to hang small racks on the inside of the door (top, center). Wrapping shallow shelves around the interior of a small pantry closet will keep your stored food and dry goods in view (right).

Replacing stationary shelves with shallow drawers or wire baskets on durable, full-extension drawer slides keeps pantry items categorized and easy to reach when pulled out (above).

APPLIANCE STORAGE Finding the right place for an appliance is often a dilemma because most larger appliances, such as food processors and bread machines, are cumbersome. An appliance garage with wooden or glass doors hides appliances at the back of the counter (below). Or you can install a lift-up shelf in a base cabinet to hold a large mixer or processor. Inserting a power head for a blender into a countertop or drawer leaves you with only the container and blades to store. Undercounter or wall mounts for coffee makers and toasters are also available.

PRODUCE PRESENTATION Replacing a solid drawer with wire, rattan, or perforated plastic baskets on drawer slides provides a handy, off-the-counter spot for potatoes, onions, or fruit (below and right). Or remove a base cabinet door and store produce in baskets on the open shelves.

BREAD BOXES You can turn any drawer that's up to 24 inches wide into a bread box with a wood, clear plastic, metal, or terra-cotta insert (right). Many inserts come with a hinged or sliding top to keep the bread fresh. Some even come with a wooden-board top so that you can cut the bread right where you store it.

HIDING THE TRASH For years the only place to hide the kitchen wastebasket was under the sink. Now trash includes recycling and is divided into categories, necessitating more than one bin (right). There are many base-cabinet trash inserts that pull out and include room for two or three bins. Some come with built-in wire bins, while others have openings for plastic garbage cans. These undercounter pullouts can also store dog and cat food (below).

HIDDEN ASSETS

Sometimes, finding room in your kitchen takes ingenuity as well as good organization. You may need to look beyond the traditional storage options to increase your kitchen's capacity. If so, it's time to take advantage of hidden air space you don't normally use.

UNDER THE UPPER Manufacturers make storage units that mount under the upper cabinets and are completely hidden when not in use. The most common are cookbook holders, knife blocks, and spice racks. If you don't have room on your countertop for a radio or CD player, choose one specially made for this often-wasted space (right).

BEHIND THE TOE KICK   Most kitchen base cabinets are raised 4 or 5 inches off the floor. Generally a baseboard, or "toe kick," runs the length of the cabinetry to keep dust from collecting below it. If you cut a section of baseboard, you can fill the space with shallow drawers that hide anything from serving dishes to silver flatware pieces to lightbulbs (above). Or you can use this space to store a folding stepladder.

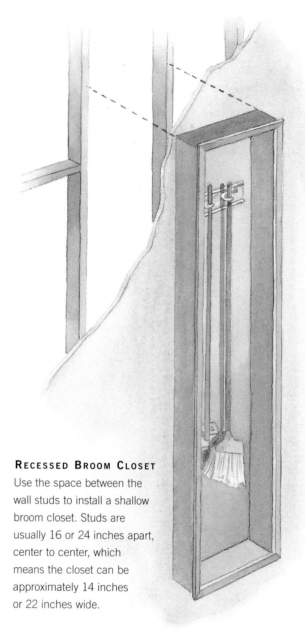

RECESSED BROOM CLOSET
Use the space between the wall studs to install a shallow broom closet. Studs are usually 16 or 24 inches apart, center to center, which means the closet can be approximately 14 inches or 22 inches wide.

IN THE WALL   In most frame construction there is a space behind the wallboard and between the studs that is about 4 inches deep. It's not big enough for a full cabinet, but it is the perfect depth for spice shelves (left), dish displays, or an ironing-board cabinet. If you have a narrow bit of wall space, this might be a good place to build a shallow cabinet for your broom and dustpan. New products are continually being introduced that use this wall space, including toaster and paper-towel cabinets.

freestanding furniture

IF YOU STILL DON'T HAVE enough room after maximizing the cabinetry in your kitchen, consider using a piece of furniture. Movable islands, cabinets, and tables come in many styles and sizes and can provide an extra work surface or additional drawers and shelves. Special features include marble butcher-block tops, bottle shelves, and dish-towel racks. Move those on casters out of the way when not in use.

Another attractive idea is to fit an antique armoire with vertical and horizontal shelves to provide more dish and food storage or to house a cookbook collection. Transform an old bedroom bureau or a library cabinet into a kitchen storage and serving area. Shallow drawers are perfect for linen storage, while deep drawers work well for big serving bowls and china.

For a contemporary look, add a metal baker's rack or modular wood shelving for more storage. Easy to assemble and relatively inexpensive, these units can stand up against a wall or be used as room dividers.

organizing the clutter

The typical kitchen has at least one cabinet or drawer that is a catchall for the equipment that doesn't have an obvious storage spot. The garlic press, eggbeater, and rolling pin compete for space in the drawer. Dry goods, canned foods, and wine bottles are difficult to find when randomly placed on a shelf. Notes, messages, and coupons left loose on the countertop are often missed or lost.

CABINET APPOINTMENTS

It doesn't have to be that way. With a little ingenuity and the right retail purchases, you can organize your dishware, dry goods, and gadgets inexpensively with ready-made products and create more space within your cabinets. Shelf maximizers, risers, and special holders increase the storage capacity of a simple shelf while bringing order to it.

PLATE RACKS Use a plate rack to keep plates from chipping or rubbing against each other. These racks provide vertical slots for plates (right).

SHELF MAXIMIZERS To double or even triple your usable space and protect your dishware at the same time, use a maximizer to store more than one layer of items on a shelf. Stack cups and saucers above dinner plates, and bowls above platters, on the same shelf (right). Maximizers come in different shapes, styles, and materials, such as wire, wood, and acrylic. Some sit on a shelf and some hang below it, providing a shallow space for flat serving dishes or linens.

CABINET PULLOUTS Transform an inefficient cabinet quickly and inexpensively with pull-out wire drawers (facing page; top), plastic baskets, or vertical dividers you can buy at home-improvement or home storage centers. While the old cabinet may take some time to clean out, these storage solutions can be installed easily and will save you time in the future.

TIERED RACKS Risers and tiered racks won't expand your shelf space but will enable you to see everything stored on the shelf. Use them for canned goods, spices, and condiments (top, right).

SPECIALTY HOLDERS If you don't have a drawer perfectly proportioned to hold foils and plastic wraps, hang them on the wall or the back of a door in a holder made for that purpose (below). Store plastic and paper bags in door-mounted holders just inside your sink cabinet.

LID HOLDERS To organize lids that don't fit anywhere else, use a lid holder. There are styles, such as door and shelf racks (right), that hold pot lids vertically so they won't get lost among your pots and pans. Lid holders also come on pull-out tracks that mount to a shelf (below, right). A large plastic mixing bowl or a square container will conveniently hold lids for plastic containers of different sizes.

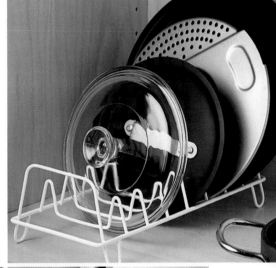

wine accommodations

MOST PEOPLE KEEP SEVERAL BOTTLES of wine in the
kitchen for either drinking or cooking. Wine is often
stored standing among other bottles and cans in a
cabinet or left cluttering the countertop. But the best
way to store wine is on its side, away from direct sun-
light and any direct heat sources, such as the stove,
oven, or dishwasher. If you have young children, store
it out of their reach.

Retail stores offer a variety of racks and bottle
holders that fit inside a cabinet or mount under a wall
cabinet. If you're buying new cabinetry, you can include
square, diamond-shaped, or circular openings for wine
bottles. When cabinet space is limited, build a freestanding wine box that stores wine safely on its side.

Whatever you use to hold wine in the kitchen,
keep in mind that it needs a stable environment to
maintain its flavor. Since temperatures in the kitchen
can fluctuate dramatically, store wine there for only
a short period.

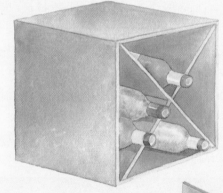

WINE CUBE
You can store a dozen bottles
of wine in this wooden box on
your countertop or floor. The
cube is made of four 12-inch-
square sheets of softwood,
such as pine or poplar, and
one back sheet cut to fit. Two
notched sheets of plywood fit
together inside the cube to
create four sections of storage.

DYNAMIC DRAWERS

With the right kinds of organizers, you can eliminate chaos in your drawers. To maximize their capacity, you should match the size of the drawer to the items you want to store. For instance, store flatware, utensils, and linens in a shallow drawer—14 to 18 inches wide for flatware and up to 30 inches wide for linens. Pots, pans, and dishes fit best in 12-inch-deep drawers. Once you determine what will go in which drawer, select an organizer that fits the drawer and contains the items in it.

UTENSIL AND FLATWARE TRAYS

These helpers separate each type of item into its appropriate compartment. Utensil trays have four or more wider compartments for serving pieces and cooking utensils. You can create your own compartments in a drawer with wood, cardboard, or plastic slats that run vertically or horizontally across the drawer's surface (above).

Most flatware trays come with compartments for knives, salad forks, dinner forks, teaspoons, and soup spoons. There are also trays that stack so that a shorter tray slides above a full-size one in a single drawer (left).

DISH AND BOWL ORGANIZERS

Different styles of organizers enable you to store plates and serving pieces inside deep drawers. A vertical-rack system protects plates from chipping. A pegboard system with removable dividers keeps stacked dishes, mixing bowls, and serving pieces in place so that they don't slide around and knock into each other in the drawer (right).

DRY AND BAKING GOODS Dry goods, such as beans and nuts, store well and are easy to locate in glass-fronted drawers lined with sheet metal. Outfitting a top drawer with plastic bins keeps flour, sugar, salt, and other baking ingredients at your fingertips (above).

LINENS Relegate everyday linens, such as place mats, tablecloths, and napkins, to wide, shallow drawers close to the serving and eating area. Use cardboard dividers cut to fit the length and width of your drawer to organize place mats, napkins, and napkin rings into compartments (above).

INSIDE A DOOR When you don't have any wall space to spare, a wall cabinet or pantry door provides a vertical surface for a message board. Line the inside or outside of the door with tackboard, pegboard, or blackboard material, and keep a small box of notepaper, pencils, chalk, or tacks on a shelf inside the cabinet. With a little extra craftsmanship, the side of an end cabinet can be fitted with tackboard, hidden behind a door (left).

THE COMMAND CENTER

The kitchen is the one room you can be certain that all family members will pass through during the course of the day. It is the obvious place for posting the week's calendar—if you are so organized—and leaving messages. But small pieces of paper, coupons, and messages are easily misplaced when they don't have a dedicated place. A message center not only organizes paperwork in the kitchen but also keeps your family in touch.

WALL SYSTEMS The easiest way to leave messages is on a blackboard or tackboard (right). These are easy to make, but if you are not so inclined, many retailers sell framed boards that do double duty as either chalk or felt pen and magnetic boards. Some boards are configured as shallow boxes, with slots on the sides to hold letters. Others have hooks below for hanging keys.

If you have an expanse of unused wall space, you can cut a hole in the wallboard and build a narrow cabinet with cubbies, drawers, and tackboard into the recessed area between the wall studs (right).

bedrooms

THE BEDROOM IS A SPECIAL PLACE in the house. It's a personal retreat where adults relax and children play. If organized properly, it also becomes a wonderful refuge from the hustle and bustle of daily life.

The best way to ensure a relaxing atmosphere is to have a dedicated spot for everything, from clothes and personal effects to books and family photos. Anything out of place will only remind you that there is work to do before you can rest. For children, disorder is a recipe for disaster. They can't amuse themselves with toys or books they can't find.

A large bedroom provides many storage options, especially if you have a big walk-in closet. A smaller bedroom requires more inventive strategies. Regardless of the size of your room, you may be surprised at how many ways you can bring order to it. On the following pages you will see how to maximize your closet space, find new places to hide things, and choose bedroom furniture that works in more ways than one.

the master bedroom

The master bedroom, unlike other bedrooms in the house, is designed for adults who work hard all day and want to rest in the evening. While some bedrooms double as an office, the master bedroom is more often used for reading, changing clothes, and sleeping. Only items related to these activities should be stored here, with the exception of art or artifacts you include to give the room its own personality.

CLOSETS THAT WORK

Ideally, you want some kind of system that enables you to hide the majority of your clothing behind closed doors. Almost every master bedroom has a closet of some kind where you can store your clothes, shoes, and accessories. Many older closets, whether they are cavernous walk-ins or narrow reach-ins with a single hanging rod, have wasted or unusable space. With the proper management, you can make either situation more efficient by installing a custom-built, do-it-yourself, or prefabricated closet system.

Limit the number of hanging rods to the amount of clothing you need to hang, and then add as many drawers and shelves as you can fit in the remaining space. In a large walk-in closet, an island of drawers with a countertop provides extra storage as well as a surface on which to fold laundry or set out accessories (left).

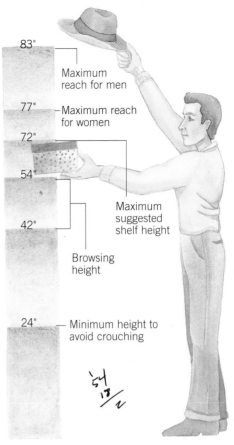

83" — Maximum reach for men

77" — Maximum reach for women

72"

54" — Maximum suggested shelf height

42" — Browsing height

24" — Minimum height to avoid crouching

IDEAL SHELF HEIGHT FOR ADULT REACH

Place regularly used items between waist height and eye level. Use lower and upper shelves for less frequently used objects. Heights are based on a 69-inch-tall man and a 65-inch-tall woman.

RANGE OF MATERIALS Depending on your budget and taste, create a closet system from wood, MDF (medium-density fiberboard), wire racks, or hanging bags. It is easy to put something together yourself, using a combination of units purchased at a home-improvement store, such as wire-basket drawers for folded clothing, hanging rods for shirts and pants, shelves for purses and shoes, and storage containers (above).

HEIGHT CONSIDERATIONS Anything you use all the time should be within your normal reach. Use the highest and lowest shelves or drawers only for items you keep stored away for unusual weather or special events. The maximum reach for the average woman is 77 inches high. For a man, it is 83 inches. You'll have to crouch down to reach anything located under 24 inches high.

SHELVES Great storage for shirts, sweaters, and handbags, shelves come in various depths to accommodate different items. They can be placed above both upper and lower hanging bars if you plan the space properly. To make a standing unit, run shelves between lengths of bars or install them at one end of the closet, using the wall for support (left). Pull-out shelves work well for keeping stacks of folded items in order.

freestanding wardrobes

IF YOUR BUDGET and closet space are limited, purchase space-saving mobile wardrobes in all wood, wood and glass, metal, or canvas over a metal frame. If you don't wish to keep a wardrobe in the open, you can hide it behind a curtain or tapestry and wheel it out when needed. Wardrobes come in different widths, with or without shelves and drawers.

Another option is to make a rotating Swedish storage tower, with shelves on one side for folded clothes and a full-length mirror on the other (right). It is an easy project for the able do-it-yourselfer, made of a three-sided rectangular box set on a rotating pedestal. The box can be framed with wooden molding to give it more style. Use a hardwood that matches other furniture in your room, stencil designs on its sides, or paint each surface a different bright color.

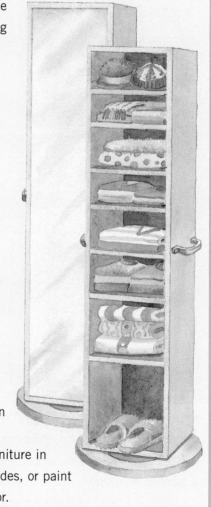

DRAWERS A tower of drawers or wire baskets provides a way to organize your folded clothes within the closet (above). Many prefabricated units allow you to combine drawers or wire baskets and shelves in a single tower.

HANGING RODS To maximize storage space, combine single rods and double rods within the same closet (left). Generally, shorter garments—blouses, short skirts, pants, and jackets—need 36 to 42 inches of hanging space. Longer ones, such as dresses, long skirts, and coats, require 66 to 69 inches.

Before determining how long your hanging rods should be, take an inventory of your clothing. How wide a space do you need for long items? How much total width do you need for short garments? Now is a good time to decide whether you need all the clothes that are hanging in the closet. If you haven't worn them in two years, give them away—or store them in the attic in case they come back into style.

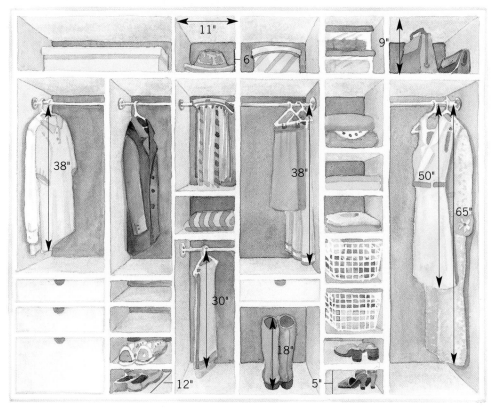

STANDARD CLOSET MEASUREMENTS
This illustration provides measurements that are based on average adult heights and styles of clothes. Check your own clothing against these measurements. The height of any hanging space should be about 4 inches greater than your longest piece of clothing.

ORGANIZING YOUR CLOSET AND DRAWERS

Having a good closet system in place is half the battle in organizing your bedroom. But how many times have you arranged your hanging clothes and refolded pants, shirts, and sweaters, only to find everything in confusion by the end of the week? There's no reason to have messy drawers, shelves, or closets with all the different organizing accessories on the market today. Give yourself a little help with some of the following ideas.

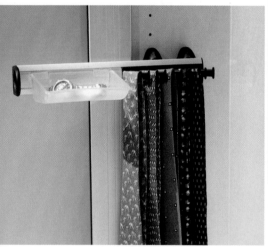

TIE AND BELT RACKS Install an extendable tie or belt rack that slides out for easy access to the back or side of your closet. You can even attach a tray that holds watches and small accessories (above). Wooden hangers with pegs, wall-mounted racks, and rows of hooks are also simple solutions. Or manage a vast tie collection with a motorized tie rack; these plug into any standard wall outlet using an AC adapter or can be operated using batteries.

DRAWER DIVIDERS To create order out of the mass of clothing and accessories in your drawers, use dividers. Multicompartment plastic or cardboard dividers come in different configurations: small squares for socks, stockings, and belts; various sizes and shapes for lingerie (below). Use clear plastic rectangular boxes to organize briefs, lingerie, or T-shirts. Cedar drawer boxes keep moths away from wool sweaters, socks, and scarves.

BOXES Open or lidded, boxes are available in different sizes to store shoes, sweaters, shirts, blankets, or just about anything else you keep in your bedroom. They are made of wood, rattan, plastic, and canvas. A lacquered pasteboard box with a lid will add a little color to your closet while protecting your items from dust (left). Clear boxes make it easy to identify contents quickly, but you can also buy opaque boxes with label holders. Use large open boxes on the floor to keep shoes in one place.

JEWELRY ORGANIZERS The obvious place to store jewelry is in a jewelry box on a bureau in your bedroom. If you don't have enough surface space for a large box, hang your earrings from a cheese grater (below) or stack your rings on an upside-down metal funnel. A shallow drawer is another convenient spot for tucking jewelry out of the way (bottom). Look for specialty inserts that fit most drawers at retail stores, or try a kitchen-drawer organizer divided into compartments.

Another option is to roll up necklaces or bracelets in padded flatware bags and tuck them among your lingerie. Or purchase a jewelry bag with multiple pockets and hang it between clothes in the closet.

SHOE RACKS Adding a shoe rack to your closet will not only keep your shoes together in pairs, it will also make them easier to find. You can set a shoe rack or cubby system on the floor under your hanging clothes (above). However, consider storing your shoes off the floor at waist height for better visibility and easier access.

If you don't have many pairs, you can line them up on a shelf between two rods of shorter hanging garments. Clear plastic boxes stacked on a shelf keep shoes visible and accessible (right). Soft plastic or canvas shoe bags that hang from your closet rod or the inside of a door save floor and wall space. Many shoe-storage systems are made to be added on to, either vertically or horizontally, as your shoe collection grows.

DUAL-FUNCTION FURNITURE

If you have done everything possible to increase your closet's storage capacity and still have more to put away, you don't have to resort to the hall closet. From headboards that stow books and photos to nightstands that stash bedtime essentials, clever bedroom furniture should serve more than one purpose if you are short on storage space.

CABINETS Antique or modern cabinets, such as armoires, add character to the room and give you more space to hide your clothes, blankets, and other personal items (below and right). They can be customized to store a television or stereo, or to double as a desk unit.

BUREAUS, DRESSERS, AND NIGHTSTANDS Chests, dressers, and bureaus are versatile storage pieces that organize and conceal

clothes and accessories. They come in just about every style and material imaginable—choose one that complements your decorating style and fulfills your storage needs.

Almost every master bedroom has some kind of nightstand for the alarm clock, lamp, and water glass. Ideally, the nightstand includes a drawer for those items you don't

want to keep on display, such as night cream, glasses, and maybe a remote control (facing page; bottom, left). If your bedside table has shelves, use stylish containers to camouflage nightstand necessities. If bookshelves flank your bed, convert one shelf at mattress height into a pull-out table and use it as your bedside table at night.

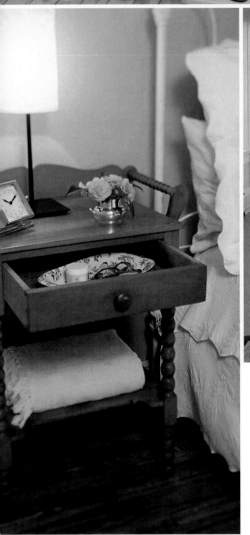

STORAGE IN A SEAT A bench or ottoman purchased or made with a hinged top that opens to reveal a storage cavity gives you more space for stowing bedroom items. A simple open bench with vertical dividers and a cushioned top functions both as a place to sit and as a stash for purses, shoes, and bedtime reading materials (left). A steamer trunk or stack of old leather suitcases placed at the foot of the bed provides great storage for folded items such as blankets or winter woolens.

BEHIND AND UNDER THE BED Headboards and frames don't have to be simple vertical planes. Many wonderful headboards incorporate both bookshelves and cubbies without taking up much extra room. And don't forget the space under the bed. Frames outfitted with drawers (above) and shallow rolling bins that tuck under the bed provide a wide storage area for larger items that might not fit easily in your closet or bureau, such as blankets and extra pillows. Keep them in breathable bags or boxes to protect against dust.

PROJECT: underbed sliding drawer

This underbed drawer is a simple sliding box on wheels. Use it as extra storage space for seasonal items or toys in a child's room. The underbed drawer does not have a top, allowing you to store things taller than 4½ inches. You can add a ⅜-inch plywood top—divided for easier access—to the drawer, if you wish. If you do not opt for a top, place items such as fine knits in sweater bags to keep them free from dust.

MATERIALS

- Two 8-ft. lengths of 1-by-6 Douglas fir boards
- One 4-by-4 sheet of ⅜-in. plywood
- 1½-in. finishing nails
- Four bed-box rollers
- One handle

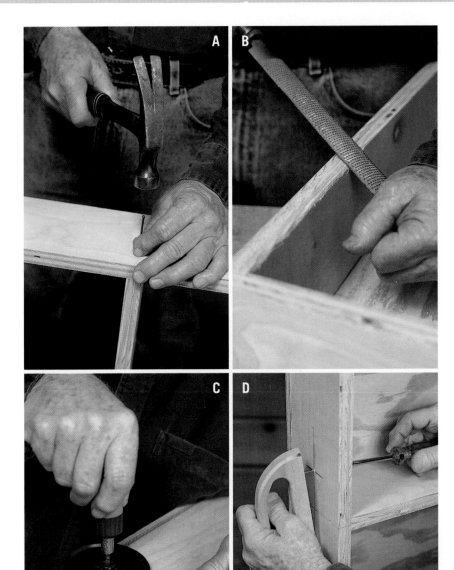

perpendicular to the faces of the two 48-inch boards, centered on the marks you just made. Nail the boards together with 1½-inch finishing nails to create the center support (**A**). Attach the two remaining pieces to the ends of the frame using butt-joint construction (see page 182 for more information on joinery). Use a file to create a rounded edge around the top of the frame (**B**) and sand it smooth. Nail the bottom of the box to the frame with 1½-inch finishing nails.

PAINTING THE DRAWER Set all nails below the surface, fill the holes with wood filler, and sand with 120-grit sandpaper. If you are going to paint the box, apply one coat of primer and let it dry. Sand again and then apply two coats of paint. For staining, sand and apply stain; sand again and apply a finishing coat such as polyurethane. See page 187 for information on finishes.

ADDING THE HARDWARE Mark both short sides of the box 3 inches from both corners and low enough so that the bed-box rollers will touch the ground when attached. Predrill the holes for the wheels at these marks and attach the wheels to the frame (**C**). Predrill holes for the handle on one long side of the box and attach the handle (**D**).

CUTTING THE WOOD Rip both of the 1-by-6s to 4½ inches wide. Cut them so that you have two boards that are 48 inches long for the sides of the drawer, and three that are 29½ inches long for the ends and a center support. Cut the 4-by-4 sheet of plywood to 31 inches wide for the bottom of the box.

MAKING THE FRAME Make a mark in the center of both of the 48-inch-long boards at 24 inches. Set one 29½-inch board on edge,

A PERSONAL SHOWCASE

When you display your favorite art, crafts, photos, and books, you give your bedroom character. Having display space also affords you the opportunity to store personal effects out in the open, where they can be found quickly and enjoyed.

HANGING IT UP Don't overlook the walls when making your storage plan. A series of hooks or a length of pegboard running along the upper third of the wall creates a system for hanging fancy hats, scarves, and even artwork. A shelf that runs up high on a wall and over doorways provides a safe display place for prized collections (left).

Take advantage of that unused space in a corner of your room with a corner cabinet topped with a hutch (below, left). The surface of the cabinet provides a perfect spot to set a television or audio system. Collectibles can be displayed on the open shelves above, and videos, CDs, and other personal items can be hidden behind doors below.

BOOKSHELVES If you have open wall space, you have room for bookshelves, either coming out from the wall or recessed into it. They can be built or purchased, depending on the size of your room and your preference. Framing a window with bookshelves adds a sense of drama to the room and also creates an alcove beneath the window that is perfect for a window seat.

Not all bookshelves need to be filled with books. Combine rows of books with breaks of open space for a personal collection of dishes, perfume bottles, or miniatures. Line shelves with pretty boxes or baskets (below), or run shelves around a painting hung in the middle of the wall.

TABLES AND OTHER SURFACES

Bedside tables, a wide headboard, bureau tops, fireplace mantels, wide windowsills, and even the top of an armoire provide surfaces for setting artifacts and framed photos (right).

DECORATIVE STORAGE Attractive storage boxes and baskets (below) are perfect hiding places for accessories such as scarves, belts, and hats if there isn't enough properly organized space in a closet or bureau.

kids' rooms

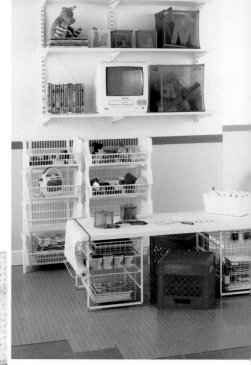

For a child, unorganized space can turn a cornucopia of toys into a nightmare of objects. What parent hasn't heard the words "I have nothing to do"? They come from a child who can't make sense of all the clutter. Most children love to sort from an early age and will keep their room clean if they have a place to put everything away. The key to kids' storage is to start with an expandable system that will work for the child as he or she grows older.

AT KIDS' HEIGHT

Children play, entertain, study, and sleep in their bedroom. They can't do any of these things well if the floor is littered with clothes and toys, and their desk and bed are in a constant state of disarray. Storage is the obvious solution to chaos, but it is efficient only if it is within your child's reach. Designing storage for kids is unique in that everything has to be stored at their height.

SHELVES   Low shelving is critical in any child's room. The maximum shelf height for a 45-inch-tall child should be 45 inches. A 62-inch-tall teenager can reach up to 66 inches. Floating bookshelves provide some flexibility (left), as they can be installed at a lower height when the child is young and moved as he or she grows taller. If you use a decorative stand-alone bookcase, place only display items on upper shelves.

One of the easiest ways to create an expandable shelf system is to use stackable storage cubes fastened together (above). As the child grows, add height to the tower.

HANDY HANG-UPS A pegboard that lines the wall or shelves with hooks (right) can hold jackets, backpacks, belts, and hats. Either can also hold laundry bags or hanging bags with compartments that are ideal for storing stuffed animals, small toys, and even shoes. Run a line of pegboard at a common chair height (about 36 inches from the floor) within your child's reach, or place a row of decorative hooks at your child's current height and raise them each year.

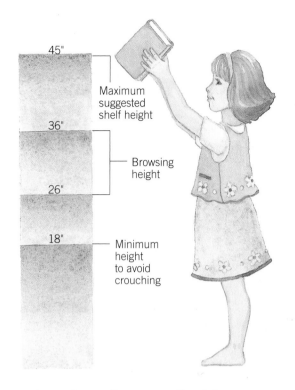

IDEAL SHELF HEIGHT FOR KIDS' STORAGE
Store toys and books on bottom shelves so they are easily accessible when children are playing on the floor. Place display items on the upper shelves. Heights are based on a 45-inch-tall child.

Since most young kids have few hanging clothes, one or two short rods set low to the ground are sufficient in the early years. Outfit the rest of the closet with drawers and shelves, altering the ratio of rods to drawers and shelves as needed (left).

ROLLING CARTS If your child has an ample closet, use a rolling cart with drawers to store toys or supplies out of sight (below). Mobile furniture allows children to control their environment to a point and move toys around to suit their immediate needs for floor space. A rolling cart with a solid top converts into a table for assembling puzzles or playing games.

A PLACE FOR EVERYTHING

While it is helpful for kids to be able to see their belongings in order to find them quickly, not everything needs to be stored out in the open. A hook or two will hang tomorrow's outfit, but the remainder of a child's clothing can be tucked away in a bureau or closet. Sporting equipment, art supplies, and games can be organized in closets, cabinets, or desks.

THE CLOSET A child's closet can be configured in much the same way as an adult's, with hanging space, shelves, and drawers. But since clothes will change in size as the child grows, choose a closet system that can be easily modified over time (right).

DESKS By the time children start school, they will need a desk where they can do their homework and keep their school supplies. The desk should have a drawer for pencils and paper and a shelf for notebooks. Since children of all ages use computers, find a desktop large enough to hold one (above). Many newer models come equipped with keyboard trays and CPU holders.

ARMOIRES Armoires that are designed for children's rooms can house a hanging rod, shelves, and drawers for clothes and linens. Use baskets with colorful liners on shelves to round up toys, books, and games (above). Some armoires come with built-in desks. The inside of a door can be lined with a blackboard or tackboard on which kids can draw or hang art.

TOY CHESTS AND BINS Toy chests are great for storing large items such as blocks, balls, and bats, and they can also serve as a bench. But avoid keeping small items in a toy chest, as they will get mixed up with everything else and be difficult to find. A frame outfitted with sliding plastic bins of varying sizes accommodates both small and large toys (right).

SPACE-SAVING BEDS

When your child's room is particularly small, every square foot of space should be used efficiently. Since the bed usually takes up the largest amount of floor space, think of it as furniture with untapped potential for extra storage. You can take advantage of the space under and around the mattress by purchasing—or building, if you're handy—a bed that has built-in drawers and shelves. With a space-saving bed, your child will have more space on the floor to play or to entertain an overnight guest.

LOFT SYSTEMS One of the best alternatives for a child's room is a loft system. These elevated beds keep the floor space underneath open for other activities. A loft system can act as a bed, closet, and work center all in one, with built-in bookshelves, a desk, a cupboard, and drawers organized below the bed platform (above). Adding a bed under the loft at a perpendicular angle will accommodate an overnight guest. Most lofts have a ladder to help the child get into bed and a guard rail to protect him or her from falling out of bed. Loft bed manufacturers also offer creative and kid-oriented features, such as an exit slide for a quick departure in the morning.

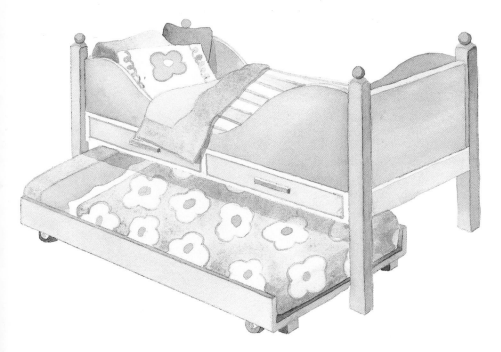

TRUNDLE BEDS If you need two beds in a room but don't have the space for them, a trundle bed is the solution. This bed takes up the same floor space as a regular twin bed but includes a second pull-out mattress under the main one. Some trundle beds sit high off the floor and include a set of drawers between the top mattress and the pull-out platform, providing a place for clothes, toys, or bed linens (left).

CAPTAIN'S BEDS A captain's bed is generally lower than a loft bed but higher than a normal one, with enough room for a deep chest of drawers or shelves below the mattress. Some beds provide drawers suitable for storing everyday clothes. Others have very deep drawers that can be used for storing seasonal clothes (right), such as heavy sweaters and snow gear, as well as board games or plastic tubs of small toys. If the drawer is deep and wide, organize it by inserting wooden dividers from front to back to create separate sections. Some taller units come with a desk that can be rolled into an opening under the bed when not in use.

HEADBOARDS A headboard with built-in shelves (left) or cupboards provides a surface for a reading light and clock, as well as storage for storybooks, stuffed animals, and collections of small toys. Keep any hard or heavy items behind securely latched cupboard doors so they can't fall on the child while he or she is in bed. Purchased in unfinished wood, a headboard can be painted and decorated to suit any interior style.

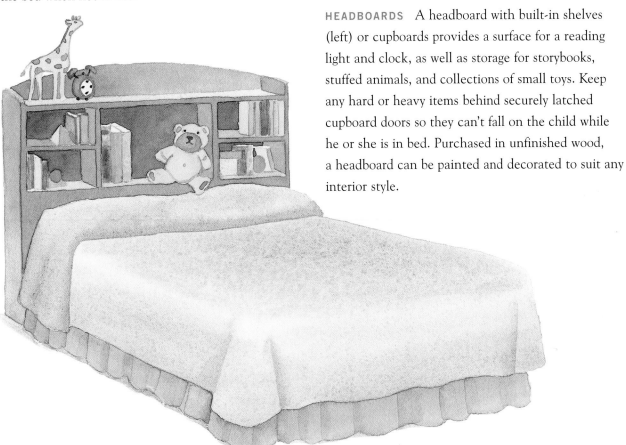

A CHILD'S GALLERY

Most children like to collect things. They bring home shells, rocks, and dried bugs to place on exhibit. They amass huge collections of books, dolls, toy cars, and stuffed animals that must be seen to be remembered. Children also create amazing artwork that has to be saved.

Sometimes it is possible to narrow down a collection when your child is at school, but in the meantime, you need a system for keeping everything on display. Here are some ideas for keeping your child's collection visible. If you store the most precious items in drawers or boxes, label the fronts with pictures or words to describe their contents.

HIGH SHELVES AND HAMMOCKS

Encircling the room with high shelves at picture-molding height (about 72 inches from the floor) creates space for displaying special items, such as figurines, dolls, stuffed animals, trains, or treasured books (above). Don't store favorite toys up high—your child will either forget about them or call on you constantly to take them down.

A colorful hammock strung across the corner of a room or along a wall is not only attractive but useful as a place to store soft toys. Unless it is high, it will be tempting to sit in, so make sure it is securely fastened into the ceiling.

ARTWORK DISPLAYS Showcase your child's newest creations or collection on the walls. One simple option is to hang a clothesline and clip laminated artwork to it with clothespins (top, left). Two other options that work well for artwork displays are shadow boxes and picture frames. Shadow boxes hold shells, miniature cars, or even doll furniture, while a frame with a back pocket makes it easy to rotate drawings and paintings.

MAGAZINE RACKS Keep a child's favorite books at the ready in a magazine rack hung on the wall (above). Racks also provide a place for older kids to file research material or homework so that it doesn't get lost in a pile on their desk or eaten by the family dog.

FLAT FILES A great place to store your child's drawings and paintings is in a flat-file cabinet. Flat files range from freestanding cabinets to custom built-in units (left), but all have wide drawers to accommodate oversize art paper. Larger cabinets have space for several years' worth of collected artwork and will fit in an amply sized bedroom. In a small bedroom, opt for a compact cabinet; it will still comfortably hold several months' worth of artwork.

KEEPING IT IN ORDER

Once you have the main furniture in place, it's time to organize all the toys and books on the shelves, or in drawers or boxes. To do this effectively, break down all your children's toys into the smallest categories possible. For instance, separate miniature stuffed animals from their larger cousins, or toy cars from trucks. When you figure out how many categories of toys your child has accumulated, you will know how many boxes, baskets, or drawer dividers to buy.

TOY TOTES   Another simple toy-containment solution is a large tote bag (above). You can use it to hold your child's favorite playmates and easily transport it from room to room. Totes are the right height for helping kids to start cleaning up their own toys.

BOXES, BASKETS, AND BINS
Clear or colored boxes or baskets with cotton liners can be stacked on the floor or on shelves and filled with sporting equipment or toys that have been sorted into categories. Label them with a word or drawing so that young children know where to return items after playing with them. Compact boxes are perfect for small blocks, cars, and doll clothes and accessories (above).

DRAWER INSERTS   Ordinarily used in the kitchen, drawer inserts can be placed in plastic boxes with lids to organize art supplies. Keep crayons and markers in one box, and paper supplies in another (left).

UNDERBED STORAGE If your child does not have a loft, captain's, or trundle bed, it's still possible to take advantage of the empty space underneath. A variety of underbed containers are available at retail stores and through catalogs (right). Before you buy, measure the space below the child's bed to make sure the container will fit.

A flat wooden platform on casters not only lets you store things under the bed, it also can be used as a roll-away hard play surface. Paint the surface with blackboard paint so that a child can use it to draw on (below).

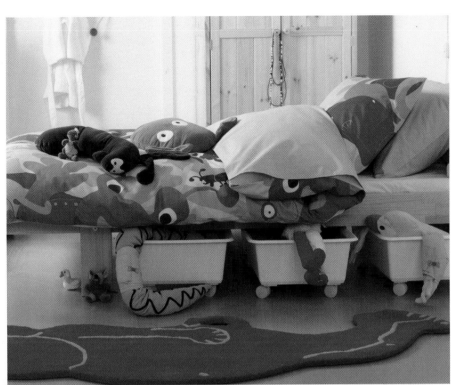

HANGING POCKETS Custom wall hangings with pockets (right) and hanging shoe bags offer storage off the floor. Attach them to the wall or the back of a door, and use them to store small items, from stuffed animals to car collections.

bathrooms

OF ALL THE ROOMS IN THE HOUSE, the bathroom has undergone the greatest transformation over time. No longer simply a utilitarian space, it's become a comfortable retreat. Today's bathrooms tend to be larger, compartmentalized, and carefully detailed. There's a place for everything, from blow-dryers and accessories to towels and toiletries, so visual clutter is reduced.

The search for additional storage has created ingenious, attractive solutions for space-shy baths, too. Overlooked niches contain skinny cabinets for storing towels; recessed between-the-studs shelves hold bottles and tubes; and wide windowsills double as shelves for decorative accessories. From powder room to master bath, you'll find fresh ideas you can use for any bathroom, whether it's spacious or compact.

bath storage

No matter how big the bathroom, storing the myriad supplies is always a challenge. Basically, there are only three ways to store belongings in a bathroom: hang them on the walls, add freestanding furniture, and build in cabinets and shelves. An effective strategy usually combines all three approaches, but the logical place to start when planning better bathroom storage is with cabinetry.

VINTAGE VANITIES Though you will lose some space to the sink and plumbing fixtures, turning a vintage piece into a vanity adds character to a bath. A fully plumbed antique cabinet hides storage behind handsome doors (above); furniture with drawers can be customized to wrap around a sink trap. Waxing the wood is one way to protect the finish of a vintage piece; for other suggestions turn to page 119.

CAPABLE CABINETS

Oversize vanities, floor-mounted and wall-mounted cabinets, and recessed (between the wall studs) units are the workhorses of bathroom storage. These cabinets help you keep decorative objects on view while hiding mundane items behind doors. Shallow cabinets take up less floor space and offer greater accessibility; reserve deeper cabinets for towels and larger supplies.

VANITY FAIR The most useful vanities come with a variety of drawers and shelves. Vertical pull-out shelves fitted with towel bars keep hand towels at the ready on either side of a sink (above). Stow bulkier objects and supplies around plumbing fixtures under the sink. To maximize efficiency in limited space, add a tilt-out drawer to serve as a clothes hamper.

If you like the antique look but prefer to use materials fashioned specially for a bath, you can find new furniture-quality vanities with fitted sinks and stone counters made to look like traditional commodes. Available at home centers and bath and kitchen stores, these attractive pieces combine old-fashioned style with today's sensible storage options.

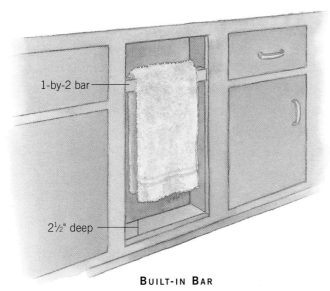

1-by-2 bar

2½" deep

BUILT-IN BAR

If your vanity lacks a towel bar, it's easy to add one just below and slightly to the side of the sink. A 1-by-2 bar allows you to grab a towel without having to search for it. Make the pocket 2½ inches deep, and finish its surfaces to match the cabinet facing. The bar itself is inset ½ inch from the cabinet front.

SIDE CABINETS Designers use pedestal, vessel, and wall-mounted sinks, as well as leggy or tapered vanities, to make rooms appear more spacious. To compensate for the loss of convenient storage, at one end of a counter add a cabinet for medicines, toiletries, and towels (above). If positioned correctly, a side cabinet can also screen the toilet (left).

RECESSED CABINETS Tucking in a cabinet between wall studs provides storage without taking up precious floor space. Shallow open shelves might display attractive bathroom items, such as soaps, guest towels, and pretty containers. A hinged door added to the recessed shelves can conceal not-so-attractive necessities. Translucent glass doors hinged to a recessed cabinet offer a happy compromise. The doors obscure neatly arranged towels at the top of the cabinet and easy-to-reach toiletries—organized in glass and metal containers—in the middle and bottom sections (below).

MEDICINE CABINETS One of the first things that comes to mind when thinking about bath storage is the medicine cabinet. It offers an easily accessible place to store numerous small items that are used frequently, such as medicines, vitamins, first-aid supplies, dental and hair products, and other items you prefer to keep out of the reach of small children. Today's medicine cabinets come in shapes, sizes, and styles to match any bath decor; some include towel racks, hooks, drawers, or pegs (above).

To add a touch of elegance to a bath, build a shallow cabinet the size of the inside measurement of a framed mirror, add adjustable glass shelves to the inside, attach the cabinet to the wall, and hinge the framed mirror onto the cabinet.

undercover helpers

THERE'S NO NEED TO GROPE around in your bathroom cabinets in search of that extra tube of toothpaste. Door-mounted hardware, pullouts, and lazy Susans work just as hard in the bathroom as in the kitchen. Slim racks mounted to the inside of a cabinet door conveniently hold small supplies. To reach storage space under the sink easily, add wire baskets or other pullouts that are installed with full-extension drawer slides or on their own special framework. And lazy Susans are storage-go-rounds that provide access to items in the far reaches of your cabinetry.

WALL CABINETS Storage of any kind is vital in baths with scant space. In larger rooms, however, the best place for storage may not be directly above or below a sink. Cabinets with drawers and shelves, placed at a convenient level next to a sink or on an adjacent wall, offer the most accessible storage for regularly used items. A bank of wall cabinets has numerous spaces for shampoo, lotion, and bath toys (above).

Hang other useful wall cabinets above a tub to display decorative bottles or over a toilet to hide workaday items such as toilet paper and cleaning supplies. Make sure that cabinets are above the head level of a seated person.

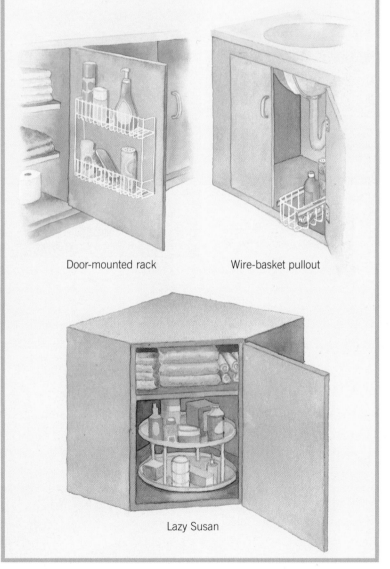

Door-mounted rack

Wire-basket pullout

Lazy Susan

HANG IT UP

When pedestal sinks and open vanities replace sink-topped cabinets, hanging storage takes up some of the slack. Well-placed hangers clear floor space and keep towels and robes easily accessible.

TOWEL HANGERS A row of hooks (right), bar-and-shelf combinations (below), stacked bars, and bars that swing back against the wall are all space savers. Heated bars that double as radiators will keep towels toasty.

You can turn almost any attractive rack into a towel bar with some creativity. Wine racks can be converted into towel tidies, with a rolled-up towel fitting into each curved bottle holder (below). Adding two racks to a bathroom wall gives you space for eight towels— a novel place for your dry whites.

CHILD'S PLAY Attaching a pegboard to the bathroom door at a comfortable height for children provides a place for them to hang up clothes or to keep a woven basket that holds their towels and tub toys (right). Allot one peg per child, and leave one or two open for extra items.

DOOR HANGERS Often, the back of the bathroom door yields overlooked storage space. Some retail hangers come with cubbies for stashing slippers, bath brushes, and towels. An over-the-door chrome and ceramic rack with multiple hooks adds instant hanging space for robes and towels (below).

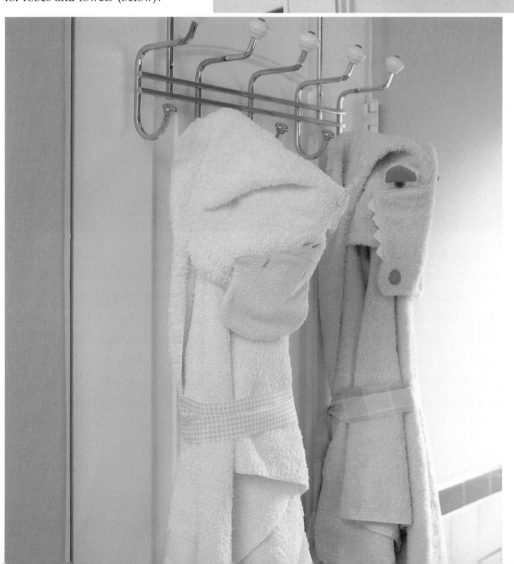

PROJECT: towel ladder

If you need additional storage for towels, consider a towel ladder that takes advantage of often-wasted vertical space. Clear plastic tubes work well as ladder rungs and have a clean, modern look. For a twist, fill their clear, hollow insides with colorful stones, potpourri, or whatever you choose to add a little splash to the bathroom. You might also substitute a variety of wooden or piping materials for the plastic tubes. Since humidity is high in bathrooms, add a water-resistant finish. Both marine resin and oil-based paints stand up well.

MATERIALS

- Two 8-ft. pieces of 1-by-3 clear Douglas fir board
- One 80-in. length of 1½-in. (outside) diameter clear plastic tube
- 1½-in. finishing nails
- Carpenter's glue
- Two 1-in.-square self-adhesive rubber feet
- Two toggle bolts
- Two 3-in. angle-iron brackets

than the 1½ inch finishing nails you will use to nail the side of the ladder to the plastic tube so that the nail will go through the tube easily.

ASSEMBLING THE LADDER Mark the center of each hole you have drilled on the 82-inch-long pieces with a pencil, and transfer that mark up to the edge of each piece. Insert the plastic tubes into the holes, being careful to line up the predrilled pinholes in the tubes with the center marks of each hole. Clamp the sides of the ladder together once all three tubes are in place. Using the center marks that you have transferred to the edge of the two ladder pieces, drill holes slightly larger than the nails. Wipe the nails with carpenter's glue and insert them into the holes, making sure that they go through the wood and into the plastic tube (B).

ATTACHING THE FEET AND BRACKETS Once you have nailed the tubes into place, attach the self-adhesive rubber feet to the bottoms of the two legs to prevent sliding (C). If you are going to paint the ladder, sand it with 120-grit sandpaper, then apply one coat of primer and two coats of paint, using a moisture-proof finish. See page 187 for information on finishes. To secure the towel ladder to the wall, use a toggle bolt through each angle-iron bracket (D). See page 181 for information on how to use a toggle bolt.

CUTTING THE MATERIALS Cut the 1-by-3 lumber to two lengths of 82 inches each for the sides of the ladder. Depending on the look that you want, you can leave the top edges straight, or round them with a file and sand them smooth. Cut the plastic tube with a hacksaw into three lengths of 25 inches each; these three pieces will be the rungs of the ladder.

DRILLING THE HOLES Using a 2-inch spade bit, make three 2-inch-diameter holes down the center of the 82-inch-long wood pieces at 24, 48, and 72 inches from the bottom. Drill each hole approximately ½ inch deep (A). Next, drill a small pinhole ¼ inch from both ends of the plastic tubes in a straight line across from each other. Make the hole slightly larger

SHELF SMARTS

When dealing with tight spaces near a sink, shower, or tub, a shelf or two can make all the difference in how a bathroom functions. Versatile shelving is a prime space saver and an inexpensive way to display towels, soaps, and other toiletries in often-overlooked areas. For example, a simple shelf mounted on brackets above a window adds unexpected storage. Open shelves fitted around one end of a bathtub hold towels within arm's reach (right). Shelves also function as a decorative element, imparting a cozy, built-in feel to this utilitarian space.

HARDWORKING SHELVES Often overlooked in modern bathrooms, shelves have great storage potential. Adding a sturdy yet inconspicuous glass shelf next to a bathtub gives you a spot for bath crystals and body scrubbers (above). A shelf with slots for cups that hold toothbrushes and toothpaste (left) is almost a necessity for sinks without a vanity or counter space.

DISAPPEARING SHELVES Now you see them, now you don't! To make a small bathroom appear more spacious, conceal built-in shelves behind a sliding door (right). The ledge over the sink holds only decorative items; bathroom essentials stay neatly hidden from view until the door is opened. Baskets, bowls, and a bucket round up toiletries and keep shelves organized.

BANJO COUNTER Extending a narrow shelf over the top of the toilet tank provides a longer surface for a small vanity and partially masks the toilet (below). And if the elements align, a banjo-shaped counter can extend beyond the toilet into the shower. This makes a small room appear larger and gives the shower a handy soap shelf.

STORING TOWELS OVERHEAD
Simple shelves built above the bathroom door provide extra storage for towels and supplies. To save space, roll towels rather than fold them.

FURNITURE ON ITS OWN

Bathroom furniture not only acts as storage, it also personalizes the space. Recycled bureaus, sideboards, and wardrobes can create a look of the past; tansu cabinets can be adapted as artful vanities. Furniture made for bathroom use is smaller in scale than conventional furniture and uses finishes that stand up to humidity. If you introduce an old piece of furniture, be sure to treat it with a durable, moisture-proof finish.

TABLES If your bathroom lacks a vanity, bringing in a small table gives you a surface for storing bath products (above). And a tiered side table offers several layers of space on which to display attractive containers and toiletries (below).

HANDY HAMPERS Select a padded hamper (above) or a storage bench to keep laundry off the floor and gain extra seating. Be sure that the hamper's lid comes equipped with safety hinges to avoid pinched fingers. When space is tight, choose a hamper that fits neatly in a corner. A removable liner makes it easy to tote laundry to the washing machine.

SEATING SPACE A stool, child's chair, or cube is a compact spot to stack towels (above) or reading material for the bathtub; it's also useful when bathing tiny tots. If you have an open vanity, add a stool or chair as a convenience. Some rolling stools have a low shelf for storage.

PORTABLE CABINETS Choose a cabinet just the right size to fit neatly into a niche or nook of your bath. Or tuck a small cabinet on top of the vanity, beside an open vanity, between his-and-her vanities (right), or next to a shower. Models with doors or drawers will keep contents dust-free. Remember that frosted glass fronts mask contents, while clear glass offers a peek inside.

wood and water

DON'T WORRY ABOUT ADDING wood furniture to a bathroom. Although hardwoods rarely were used in that humid environment in the past, today's durable finishes have made them handsome choices for bathroom cabinetry. Some hardwoods fare better than others in adapting to dampness; your best choices are ash, cherry, hickory, maple, oak, and walnut.

Manufacturers and installers apply finishes to new furniture and built-ins that keep moisture from penetrating the wood while still allowing it to expand and contract. If you're recycling an old wood piece, protect it with a polyurethane finish or a marine-type penetrating resin.

ORGANIZERS AND ACCESSORIES

Storing appliances and supplies where they are needed takes ingenuity, but handsome organizers help customize bathrooms. Interesting baskets, boxes, trunks, trays, bottles, and jars also add personality to what could be a sterile space (right).

VANITY INSERTS Slip plastic inserts into drawers to organize makeup and brushes (above). Special hinges attach a molded tray inside the false drawer front of a vanity, creating room for toothbrush and toothpaste. Plastic cups in adhesive holders fit flat against the inside of a medicine cabinet door to hold brushes, combs, and other items.

appliance adjuncts

AMONG THE HOST OF STORAGE AIDS designed for storing small bathroom appliances are wall- or door-mounted vinyl pouches (sold as closet organizers) and wire racks and baskets. If grooming appliances have hanging loops, use wall racks with hooks or pegs, or screw cup hooks to the underside of a shelf. To keep from damaging power cords, don't wrap them around appliances. Instead, coil cords into loose loops and stuff them into empty bathroom tissue tubes. Always wait until appliances are cool before putting them away.

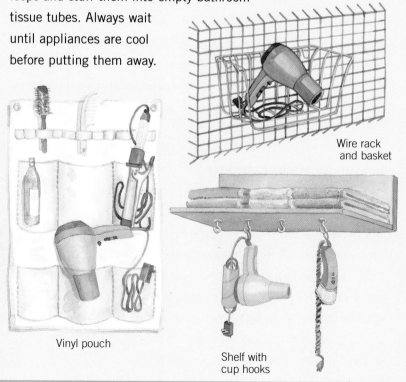

Wire rack and basket

Vinyl pouch

Shelf with cup hooks

BATH CATCHALLS A generous caddy slipped over the showerhead holds soaps and shampoos. Some models add hooks for washcloths, scrub brushes, and loofah sponges. A caddy that you slide over the top of the tub keeps bath salts, soaps, and lotions at hand. Tucking shower essentials—and tub toys—into the small pockets of a plastic shower curtain makes it easy to grab what's needed (right).

TISSUE TIDIES You'll always know when it's time to buy more when you place a generous wicker basket or a covered hamper beside the toilet to hold extra tissue rolls (right). A hamper can also conceal other personal hygiene products.

ORGANIZER WALL In a bath without a vanity, a room divider becomes a wall of storage (left). To make best use of the space, the sizes of the open-topped wicker organizers determine the proportions of the cabinet housing them. Grouping similar baskets in a variety of sizes lets you cluster towels, toiletries, cosmetics, appliances, and other bath items without a clutter of containers.

home offices

IN A HOME OFFICE, STORAGE CONSIDERATIONS depend on where the space is located and how it is used. If your office is separate from the rest of the house, you have more flexibility than if it is located in a room used for other purposes, such as the kitchen, the family room, or a bedroom. If you operate a business from your home, your storage needs are greater than if you use the office solely for paying bills, planning menus, and keeping your household activities organized.

Your unique situation determines the kind and quantity of storage products you need. With adequate storage, you can spend your time in the office working rather than searching for pen and paper or misplaced files and documents.

home-office basics

The key to creating an efficient office, whether it is separate from the rest of the house or tucked into a room that serves another purpose, is to start with good, basic office furniture. The home-office market has grown considerably, and there are modular systems and stand-alone pieces of furniture to fit any office scenario.

WORKING IN BORROWED SPACE

When you set up your office in a room used for other purposes, the most important principle is to blend the work space with its surroundings and keep it free of office clutter. This is not as difficult as it sounds if you choose the right pieces for your work area. For example, if you are adding a workstation to your kitchen or great room, check out cabinets that come with matching desks and wall shelves (top, right).

OFFICE ARMOIRES One of the best ways to disguise your office completely is to enclose it within an armoire or cabinet (right), which can be purchased to suit almost any interior decor. The doors open to expose a desk surface, a keyboard tray, file space, and bookshelves. Some are equipped with a shelf under the desktop for storing a CPU. Armoires and cabinets are a bit limited for a full-scale business operation but provide the storage needed for telecommuting and household management.

CLOSET OPTIONS When you are carving out space for an office in a guest room, consider hiding your desk inside the closet (right). A 24-inch-deep closet is well suited for this purpose. The only modification you may have to make is to add an electrical outlet. Start with a stock desktop; these are available in sizes ranging from 20 to 36 inches deep and 28 to 70 inches long. Customize the space with a keyboard tray, shelving, a file cabinet, letter boxes, and a message board.

CREATIVE FILING One limitation of having an office in a dual-use room is that it is difficult to find a place for the invaluable but often unattractive file cabinet. You can buy file cabinets disguised as furniture—footstools, side tables, and rattan or wooden boxes—to match the style of your room (below).

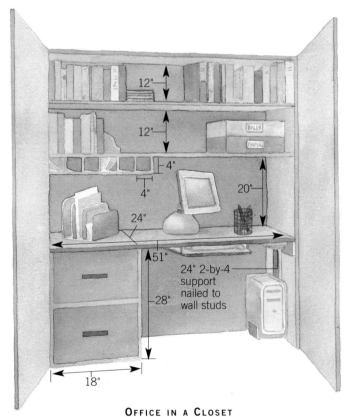

OFFICE IN A CLOSET

Create an office in an empty reach-in closet with only a file cabinet, a desktop, and bookshelves. When you're finished working, you can shut the doors and your office is completely hidden.

A ROOM OF ITS OWN

If you have a room used only for business, you won't have to worry about camouflaging your office. In this case, invest in furniture that offers maximum storage options. What you select depends on the nature of your work.

Evaluate how much open desk space you need to work comfortably, the amount of material you file, how many resource items you store on shelves or in cabinets, and what special functions you perform. For example, an architect or contractor needs a large, flat surface to display plans and a special filing system to store them. A business consultant may require less desktop space but need more vertical file cabinets.

No matter what kind of business you conduct, it is a given that you will always need more storage than you think. Plan for change by purchasing furniture that is flexible enough to grow with your business.

STOCK DESK UNITS Today's manufactured desks range from a simple work surface (left) to a desk that includes a keyboard tray, a CPU holder, a printer shelf, pencil and file drawers, or a desktop hutch (above). Desks come in metal, wood, or composite with different veneers to suit your style. A stock unit will not be easy to add on to seamlessly if your needs change, since it can be difficult to match the veneer of your existing unit.

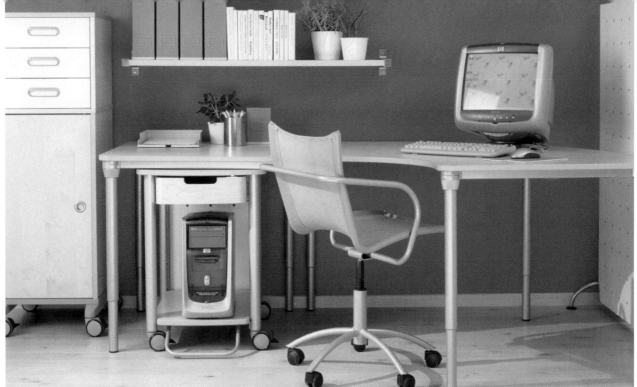

MODULAR OFFICE FURNITURE

If you purchase modular units, you can alter the desktop's length and configuration, as well as add new pieces, such as drawers and wall storage, when your needs change or grow. Matching mobile carts (above) and cabinets provide additional work surfaces when they're rolled out from under the desktop.

If you're on a strict budget, create your own modular system using bits and pieces from a variety of sources. A desktop can be constructed out of an old door or countertop and supported by metal file cabinets or tool chests (right). A kitchen or glass patio table serves the same purpose. Follow the theme and use baskets or boxes to create filing systems, and old ceramic mugs to organize pencils and pens. Office furniture does not have to be modern to be efficient, as long as it has ample storage.

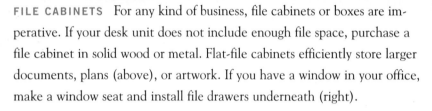

FILE CABINETS   For any kind of business, file cabinets or boxes are imperative. If your desk unit does not include enough file space, purchase a file cabinet in solid wood or metal. Flat-file cabinets efficiently store larger documents, plans (above), or artwork. If you have a window in your office, make a window seat and install file drawers underneath (right).

murphy beds

WHEN YOUR HOME OFFICE DOUBLES AS GUEST QUARTERS, one of the best innovations on the market is the modern Murphy bed. Not only is a Murphy bed more comfortable than most sofa beds, it folds into a wall cabinet that takes up no more floor space than a standard bookcase. Most cabinets can be matched to your office

furniture for a sleek, integrated look. Murphy bed manufacturers offer full-height cabinets to flank the bed, with drawers, shelves, wardrobes, or even nightstand-height pull-out shelves. Some manufacturers give you the option of ordering a pull-down table built into the exterior panel, which can increase your work space considerably. Murphy beds come in all standard bed sizes, and many support conventional mattresses.

within arm's reach

Most of your time in the office is spent sitting at a desk, which means that all the items you use regularly need to be within reach of your chair. None of the daily tools of your trade—pencils, paper, envelopes, stamps, files, printer, or fax machine—should be farther than 2 feet away from that chair.

CLOSE FOR COMFORT

Your desktop may provide enough space to store all those things you want accessible, especially if it is wide and has a return to the side. If your office has minimum desk space, consider investing in a laptop computer that folds flat or tucks away when not in use (top, right). But remember that clutter builds up very easily on any flat surface unless you have a dedicated place for each item that accumulates there.

COMPUTERS AND PERIPHERALS

You can purchase a CPU-tower holder that mounts under your desktop, if your desk unit doesn't include one. A monitor can sit on a stand, creating room below it for mail, work in progress, or other important papers.

Store peripherals, such as printers, scanners, and fax machines, on pull-out shelves built for that purpose (right). Mobile carts that fit under your desk when not in use are suitable for both peripherals and CPUs.

REFERENCE BOOKS AND FILES

A dictionary, a thesaurus, phone books, and textbooks are best located on the desktop, on shelves you can reach easily from your chair, or in a wall cabinet above the desk (left). You can further organize an existing wall cabinet by adding cubbies and horizontal dividers that fit different sizes of books and paper. Keep frequently used files at your fingertips by storing them in a file drawer to the side of your chair or in a box or basket on your desktop (above).

ESSENTIAL SUPPLIES Use the pencil drawer just below the desktop for office essentials, such as pencils, pens, stamps, and paper clips. Most single desks include this shallow drawer, and many modular units enable you to install a drawer anywhere under the desktop. If there is room next to your desk, purchase a cabinet with a pencil drawer on top and file drawers or shelves below it (left). If you don't have a drawer, put your small supplies in a lidded container on an open shelf within easy reach from your chair (above).

all wired up

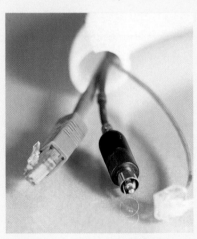

CONNECTING THE WIRES TO YOUR OFFICE EQUIPMENT is easy. Finding a place for them to hide where they won't tangle up and interfere with your feet is the real challenge.

There are many different ways to organize the clutter of electrical wires. If you have a desktop with a built-in wire-management system, your choice is obvious. If not, you can create your own system.

Assuming that several wires are plugged in to the same power strip with surge protection, you can run them together up a leg of your desk and hold them there with Velcro strips, electrical wire ties, hook and loop straps, or even phone-wire staples. Also available are plastic channels or conduit that affix to the leg or side of your desk and hide the wires completely. Once they are under your desktop, direct the wires through plastic troughs or wire baskets so that no wire hangs below the underside of your desk.

If you prefer to have the wires come up directly behind each piece of equipment, you can drill holes in the desktop at appropriate places. The holes need to be big enough for the plug to fit through easily. Finish the rough holes with plastic or wood grommets. Grommet caps cover all but the wire itself so you have no holes visible in your surface.

in plain sight

You may not be able to reach all the materials you use in your office without leaving your chair. However, if you keep the important ones within your line of vision, you'll be able to find them quickly when you need them.

SHELVES A bookshelf system is a must for displaying the books, periodicals, and computer disks you keep in your office. The system can consist of built-in shelves (below), boxes with adjustable shelving, or shelves supported by brackets on tracks (right). Many modular office systems include bookshelves as an option.

MAGAZINE POCKETS AND RACKS
Mounting a magazine rack on the wall makes important periodicals easy to locate. These racks are available in many interesting styles and materials, ranging from nylon mesh (above) to wood and rattan.

MESSAGE BOARDS Keep important notices on message boards, which come in all shapes and sizes. You can purchase framed tack- or magnet boards, or line an empty wall with sheets of tackboard material. Clip-style (below) and magnetic message boards are available at home stores, but an inexpensive option is to nail several metal clips to the wall and hang notes from them. Or cover a piece of corkboard with fabric, and tack ribbons across it; slide messages under them (bottom, right).

LETTER CUBBIES AND WIRE-RACK SYSTEMS Keep mail visible in cubbies that run under bookshelves or are incorporated into a shelving unit. Having several slots enables you to sort bills according to when they need to be paid, and the slots can hold certain pieces of mail for future attention (above). A wire-rack system that mounts on the wall (below) also keeps letters, bills, binders, and important files in clear view.

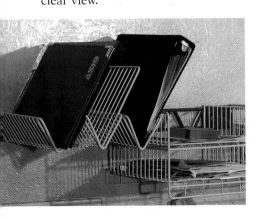

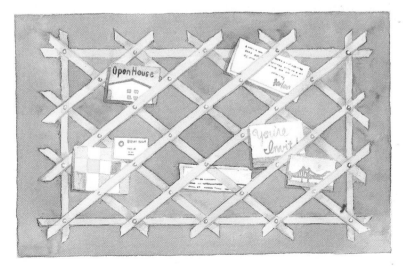

FABRIC MESSAGE BOARD

Fashion an attractive message board out of a sheet of corkboard, a piece of fabric, and ribbons. Pull the fabric tight around the board and staple it to the back. Crisscross ribbons in an interesting pattern across the front, and attach their ends to the board with thumbtacks.

a place for everything

If you develop a smart organizational system in your office for supplies and equipment, they will be easy to find. Since the market for home-office organizing products is growing all the time, you can find a storage box or tray for every type of office accessory in every style and material imaginable. Keeping your office as stylish as the rest of your house is important, since you may spend more time there than anywhere else.

DESKTOP ORGANIZERS Desktop trays and letter organizers come in both horizontal and vertical styles in materials such as metal mesh, wire, galvanized steel, plastic, rattan, wood (below), colored cardboard, and even leather. Some organizers combine horizontal trays with vertical slots so that you can store paper, mail, and file folders in the same spot; some include small holders for pens, paper clips, and business cards.

DESKTOP HUTCHES Placing a hutch on your desk keeps paper-work and small items organized and off your desktop without having to attach something to the wall. Many hutches have drawers for files and space for stationery (above). Most hutches are no deeper than the width of a sheet of paper—about 9 inches—leaving room in front of them on the desktop to work.

PEN CANISTERS An attractive addition to your desktop is a pen holder with individual slots that keeps writing utensils at your fingertips (facing page; top, right). If you want to add a little color to the room, find a bright coffee mug to serve this purpose.

CDs AND DISKS Computer disk and CD storage is available in many styles, from holders that sit on your desktop (near right) to those that mount on a wall. If your office needs a little pizzazz, look for CD holders in bright colors and unusual shapes.

DRAWER DIVIDERS A great way to separate pens, tape, sticky pads, paper clips, staples, and all the other items you store in a desk drawer is to add dividers. Some drawers come with inserts and dividers, but you can use anything from loaf pans (below) to small open boxes.

MAGAZINE BUTLERS You can hold up to a year's worth of periodicals in a magazine butler (right) so individual issues are easy to find and won't fall over on your bookshelf. The least expensive come in colored cardboard, but you can find others in materials to match the rest of your office accessories.

CONTAINERS Available in all sizes and materials ranging from sturdy cardboard (above) to rattan to galvanized metal, fashionable containers organize supplies such as colored paper, paints, pens, files, and anything else you might store in your office. Purchase stackable containers that fit below your desk, on your bookshelves, or in a closet.

PROJECT: desktop hutch

This 42-inch-long hutch is a convenient storage spot for office supplies that you want near you on the desk. It will hold stacks of 8½-by-11 paper and stationery, files, large envelopes, CDs, books, bills, and outgoing mail. It also features built-in bookends on the top. If you have a hardwood desk, you might want to make the hutch of the same wood;

or use MDF (medium-density fiberboard) or pine if you plan to paint it.

MATERIALS

- **One 4-by-8-ft. sheet of ¾-in. plywood**
- **1½-in. finishing nails**

CUTTING THE WOOD Rip the plywood into four lengths, each 10 inches wide by 8 feet. Next, cut the ripped boards so that you

have the following lengths: two pieces, 40½ inches (top and bottom); two pieces, 18 inches (sides); three pieces, 12¾ inches (the vertical dividers); four pieces, 9 inches (shelves); one piece, 11½ inches (shelf).

NAILING THE DIVIDERS AND SHELVES TOGETHER Start by marking lines with a pencil on the inside of one of the $12\frac{3}{4}$-inch boards at $3\frac{1}{4}$, 4, $6\frac{1}{2}$, $7\frac{1}{4}$, $9\frac{3}{4}$, and $10\frac{1}{2}$ inches from the left side of the board. Transfer these marks to one of the 18-inch-long boards, lining up the edge of the $12\frac{3}{4}$-inch board $\frac{3}{4}$ inch in from the edge of the 18-inch-long board to allow room for the bottom piece when it is attached (**A**).

Place three of the 9-inch shelves between the marks you made on the inside of the 18-inch board—the shelves should be $2\frac{1}{2}$ inches apart. The shorter end of the 18-inch board will eventually attach to the bottom of the hutch. Nail two $1\frac{1}{2}$-inch finishing nails through the outside of the side board (the 18-inch board) into the edges of the 9-inch shelves (**B**). If it's helpful, draw lines on the outside of the 18-inch board to guide the nails.

Attach another 9-inch shelf to another $12\frac{3}{4}$-inch divider so that it is 5 inches from the top. Butt this divider against the three shelves you already attached to the side board, making sure the longer end of the divider lines up with the mark that is $\frac{3}{4}$ inch from the edge on the bottom of the side board. Nail through the divider and into the shelves (**C**).

Now nail the $11\frac{1}{2}$-inch shelf into the last $12\frac{3}{4}$-inch divider so that the shelf is $6\frac{1}{4}$ inches from the top of the divider. Butt this piece to the divider with the 9-inch shelf so that the shorter end faces the bottom. Line up its bottom edge up with the previous divider and nail in place.

ATTACHING THE BOTTOM AND TOP Turn the hutch on its side and nail one of the $40\frac{1}{2}$-inch boards into the three dividers, butting into the 18-inch side board on the left. This is now the bottom of the hutch.

Turn it right side up and butt the second 18-inch side into the bottom of the hutch on the right side. Nail it in place. Place the other $40\frac{1}{2}$-inch piece on top of the dividers and nail it in place through the dividers (**D**). The side pieces will extend 4 inches past the top piece; these are the bookends. Nail through the 18-inch sides into the edge of the top for extra strength.

FINISHING THE HUTCH Set all nails below the surface, fill the holes with wood filler, and sand with 120-grit sandpaper. Apply stain and finish, or primer and paint. See page 187 for information on finish options.

chapter eight

utility rooms and bonus spaces

UTILITARIAN SPACES LIKE LAUNDRY ROOMS and mudrooms seldom receive the organizational attention they deserve, which is odd when you consider how often they're used. But a little planning can turn these hardworking zones from centers of clutter to models of efficiency.

The rooms can even serve multiple functions, which is essential when space is tight. A mudroom may double as a grooming center for the family pets and a storage room for out-of-season sports gear. An overhead rack in a laundry room can be used for drying flowers as well as clothes, and the sink area is perfect for potting plants. A sewing center may share an ironing board and fold-down table.

Stairway landings, hallways, and closets also harbor underused space. With a little creativity, these bonus areas can be transformed into craft centers, study nooks, or even sleeping spaces.

laundry rooms

Lose the laundry blues by organizing the washing and drying space into sorting, folding, and ironing centers, each equipped with supplies necessary to perform the task. Key elements include ample storage for detergent; a utility sink for items that need washing by hand; a rack or clothesline for drip-drying; a table or a 36-inch-high counter for folding; water-resistant, easy-to-clean work surfaces; and adequate task lighting.

LAUNDRY 101

Utilize space above, below, beside, and between the washer and dryer. Some newer models come with a storage drawer below the machine (top, right). Provide plenty of storage accessories for sorting, hooks for hanging, shelves for stacking (below), and laundry caddies for transporting clothes. Add a step-on can for disposing of lint, a see-through container for items retrieved from pockets, and a bulletin board for tacking up laundry care tags.

HIDING THE LAUNDRY When a washer and dryer are tucked into an alcove, add shelves, wall cabinets, or cubbies for supplies. Cover it all up with easy-to-open bifold, sliding, or pocket doors, or with seamless cabinet doors that offer access to each area independently. If a front-loading pair—either side by side or stacked—are nestled into a cabinet run, mask them with doors that match their surroundings (above). Adjacent cabinets or drawers might house an ironing board, a pull-out sorting table, and a tilt-down clothes bin.

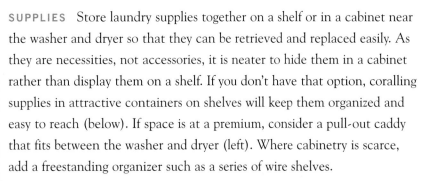

SUPPLIES Store laundry supplies together on a shelf or in a cabinet near the washer and dryer so that they can be retrieved and replaced easily. As they are necessities, not accessories, it is neater to hide them in a cabinet rather than display them on a shelf. If you don't have that option, coralling supplies in attractive containers on shelves will keep them organized and easy to reach (below). If space is at a premium, consider a pull-out caddy that fits between the washer and dryer (left). Where cabinetry is scarce, add a freestanding organizer such as a series of wire shelves.

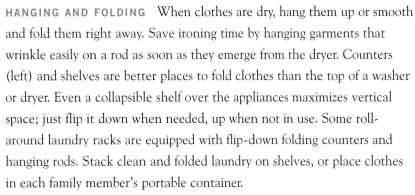

HANGING AND FOLDING When clothes are dry, hang them up or smooth and fold them right away. Save ironing time by hanging garments that wrinkle easily on a rod as soon as they emerge from the dryer. Counters (left) and shelves are better places to fold clothes than the top of a washer or dryer. Even a collapsible shelf over the appliances maximizes vertical space; just flip it down when needed, up when not in use. Some roll-around laundry racks are equipped with flip-down folding counters and hanging rods. Stack clean and folded laundry on shelves, or place clothes in each family member's portable container.

COLLECTING AND SORTING

Once dirty clothes are collected and sorted, washing them becomes a cinch. Ideally, family members should carry their own laundry to and from the washer and dryer. Portable receptacles placed in their bedrooms or baths remind them of the chore (left).

Pull-out bins (above), hampers, or baskets in the laundry room encourage family members to separate clothes. Label or color-code hampers for lights and darks. If you have space, add organizers for items like hand-washables and permanent-press garments.

BUILT-IN SORTER

One option for sorting clothes is to build a cabinet with a single deep drawer under a counter. Use plywood dividers to partition the drawer into compartments for whites, colors, and permanent press. Another divider could be added for towels and sheets. Install the drawer with heavy-duty drawer slides.

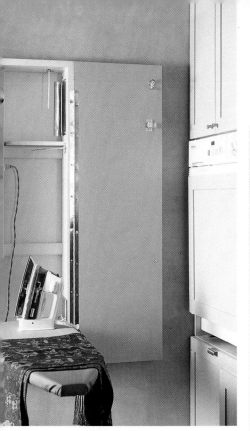

IRONING CENTER An iron and a full-size ironing board that pulls down for use might be stored inside a wall-mounted or recessed cabinet (above). If the cabinet is equipped with a light and an electrical outlet for the iron, make sure there is a safety switch to cut power when the door is closed. If you're short on space, choose an ironing board that hangs over a door. Boards come with an array of chic covers, but solids make it easier to see wrinkles.

LAUNDRY CHUTE A built-in laundry chute transports clothing from an upper floor down to a laundry room (right). A pull-out hamper is situated underneath the end of the chute to catch clothing as it drops through. When it's time to put in a load of laundry, the hamper rolls easily over to the washing machine.

where to locate a laundry chute

A LAUNDRY CHUTE directs dirty clothes from your home's main or second floor to a laundry center in the basement or garage below. You can locate the chute opening in an inconspicuous but handy spot—inside a clothes closet in the master bedroom; in a wall, with a hinged or flap door; or inside a bathroom cabinet. To reduce the risk of small children falling into the chute, be sure that the opening is raised high above the floor and measures no more than 12 inches across.

The best time to construct your laundry chute is when you're designing or remodeling your house. Build the chute from sheet aluminum, 18-inch-diameter furnace heating duct, or plywood, depending on your local building codes.

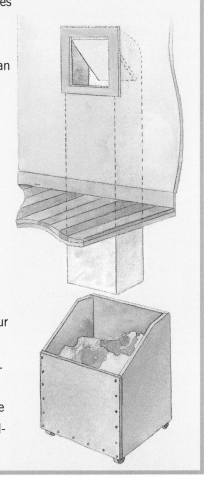

mudrooms

A laundry room often shares space with a mudroom. This family loading and unloading zone near the back or side door probably sees more in-and-out traffic than the front entry. Everyone stops here at least long enough to park book bags, shed muddy shoes, and drop off tennis racquets. When outfitted with carefully planned storage systems, effective mudrooms neatly capture back-door clutter and much more.

RACKS, SHELVES, AND BENCHES
Instead of letting a mudroom become cluttered, take advantage of its potential. Counters, tables, and benches are storage pieces that collect and organize both day-to-day and seasonal items. When outfitted with a bench surrounded by four generously sized cubbies, a makeshift mudroom area near the back door efficiently stores jackets, purses, dog leashes, and extra bags of dog food (below).

Many cost-effective storage solutions are tailored specially for utility spaces. You'll find a wealth of inexpensive storage aids, such as wall-mounted racks for boots (top, right), shelves for shoes, and hangers for coats (below, right), in catalogs and at home centers and container stores.

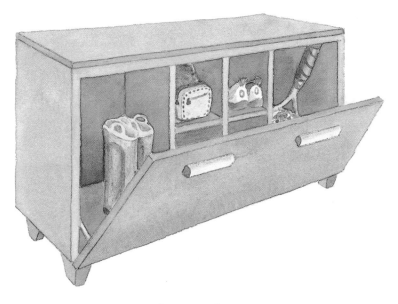

CATCHALL CABINET

When a utility space opens onto a deck, patio, or yard, shoes and gardening gear tend to pile up by the door. An easy-to-make drop-front cabinet helps control the mess. The cubbies are suitable for extra boots, book bags, or bulky outdoor items.

PET LOCKER If you need more than just a hook for Fido's leashes, buy or build a box with a hinged door to hide your pet's necessities (above). Divide the interior into compartments for essentials, such as food, shampoo, medications, and toys. Add hooks for collars, leashes, brushes, and combs, and perhaps a rod to hold a roll of pickup bags. A freestanding box could also round up feeding bowls, food, towels, and toys. For convenience, locate the locker near a laundry sink where your pet may at least tolerate a bath.

LOCKER ROOM A built-in wall cabinet is one of the best ways to organize an active family's sports clothing and gear, hats, jackets, shoes, pool towels, and the like (left). You might add a pull-out rod for hanging wet clothes and an accompanying bench or stool for unloading bags or changing shoes.

hobby and craft centers

When utility rooms double as hobby and craft areas, careful planning is necessary to maximize the space. At a minimum, these areas need easy-to-clean surfaces, work space, and appropriate storage: shelves for flowerpots; wide, flat drawers for art supplies; and wall-mounted organizers for sewing supplies. Also check stores that cater to your hobby for specialized storage items.

SUPPLY COLLECTORS

Decide which supplies you want on display and which should be stowed away behind cabinet doors. If you need to keep projects in progress spread out, locate a counter or worktable in an out-of-the-way corner of the room.

GARDEN SPOTS In a mudroom, a storage cabinet encloses a sink, providing space for flowerpots and tools used in the garden. An attractive hanging shelf keeps vases and accessories in clear view (top).

A laundry room can double as a place where blossoms become bouquets. It has all the requisites: plenty of counter space, convenient access, and a water source. A metal countertop around a sink makes an ideal place to cut and arrange flowers; open shelves nearby hold vases and supplies (left). The table serves as work space for both laundry and craft projects.

UNDER WRAPS A compact gift center squeezes into the open space between a washer and dryer (below). The counter becomes a convenient surface for wrapping packages, and a drawer below holds scissors, tape, pens, and labels. Long rolls of wrapping paper sit on a shelf in the utility cupboard above. Another shelf might be reserved for small gifts. A wall-mounted wire rack efficiently dispenses ribbons and bows.

CRAFT ITEMS Thread, ribbon, scissors, and other craft items you want to reach from a seated position can be hung on a wall-mounted organizer above your chair or in a cabinet that sits on or next to the desk (above). Larger items, such as fabric squares for quilting, drawing tools, and paints, can be stored in labeled plastic boxes stacked next to your desktop or on shelves above it.

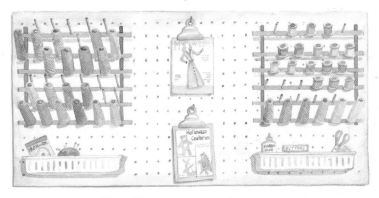

WALL-MOUNTED CRAFT ORGANIZER

A wall organizer keeps thread, needles, scissors, sewing patterns, and other craft accessories in order so they are always easy to find.

bonus spaces

Make the most of every space in your home, including hallways, stairway landings, and closets. It takes just a little creativity to add storage space in a previously overlooked spot. Not many square feet are needed to add a work space, a hidden nook for valuables, or a cabinet in a hallway (right).

STORAGE FINDS

Shelves, cabinets, and closets can be tailored to fit neatly into hallways, niches, alcoves, and other small sites. Narrow shelves make use of forgotten wall space; shallow cabinets organize art supplies, gift wrapping, or games; and linen closets contain much more than their name implies.

SLEEP SPACE Turn an alcove between two rooms into a quiet refuge for reading or naps (above). In a pinch, it's a pleasant place to

put up a slumber party guest. Add drawers underneath the bed and shelves at each end of the alcove for display and storage space.

WORK NOOK A small site offers hidden potential for carving out a work space. A communication center is tucked into a corner off the hall (right). Bright red paint delineates the space and adds a touch of drama. Shelves hold a phone, books, and other items needed to keep in touch with friends and schedule family appointments and outings.

LINEN CLOSETS Naturally attracting overflow from bedrooms and baths, linen closets are invaluable. When properly organized, the closet space can store far more than sheets and towels; it can also be the place where you look for toiletries, bath tissue, cleaning products, and personal care items. A rolling cart allows you easy access to supplies, and door hooks keep bathrobes at the ready (top, right).

Store items that are seldom used or dangerous to children on high shelves, small items that are hard to spot at eye level, and light but large items on bottom shelves (above). Washcloths and towels are most conveniently kept at waist level. If you store towels and sheets in stacks, placing the folded side out makes it easier to grab them. Some closet organizers suggest folding towels in sets with washcloths, and sheet sets inside matching pillowcases or shams.

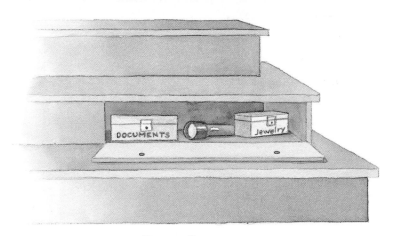

HIDDEN SPACE
Sometimes extra space is literally at your feet. Adding a hinged door to a stair riser lets you store valuable papers or small treasures under the stair. A finger pull allows easy access to secluded items without obstructing passage.

garages, attics, and basements

GARAGES, ATTICS, AND BASEMENTS are the ideal places to store all those things you use seasonally, put aside for the future, or can't fit anywhere else. Unfortunately, many things there just gather dust until you prepare for a move or a major yard sale. Those forgotten objects take up space that could be dedicated to other purposes, such as parking, a playroom, or a workshop.

These spaces can be organized so that they provide all the extra storage you need. Since they are not formal living areas, they don't have to look fancy, and they can be outfitted rather inexpensively with a variety of storage options. You can reinstall old kitchen cabinets on the walls, hang equipment on hooks from the walls and ceiling, and use recycled materials for shelving. Inexpensive open shelving units made of wire or wood are ideal for garages. More expensive—and aesthetically pleasing—storage systems are also available. The key is to store everything so that it can be found easily, without having to disrupt the rest of the room.

front and center

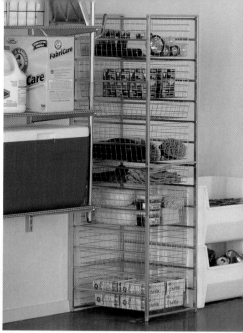

In many a garage, attic, or basement, the most accessible objects are those that were last deposited. This is a recipe for chaos and makes it impossible to find anything quickly. When rearranging your space, separate items into long-term, seasonal, and current storage categories. Then dedicate a place within easy reach for items you use regularly, such as dry goods, food, sporting equipment, and tools.

DRY GOODS AND FOOD

Buying food and dry goods in bulk saves both time and money. But finding a place to store the oversize boxes of cereal, the flats of canned goods, and the giant containers of detergent presents a problem. You want to reach these without pushing anything else aside. Store them close to the door, either on open shelves or in cabinets, keeping heavier items between waist and chest height (left). If you store bulk goods such as flour and sugar, use large plastic containers with secure lids to keep moisture, insects, and rodents out.

TIERED RACKS If you keep a supply of canned goods in this area, use tiered racks or risers on your shelves for easy identification.

STACKING BINS AND WIRE DRAWERS Use metal frames with wire drawers or stacking bins in conjunction with shelving to organize a garage or basement wall for dry goods and food (top).

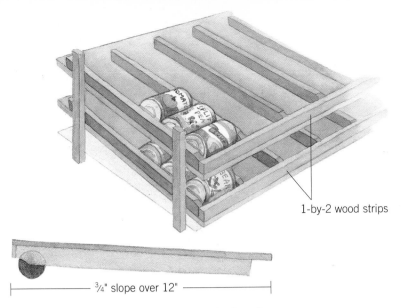

1-by-2 wood strips

¾" slope over 12"

SLOPING SHELVES FOR CAN STORAGE

Food shelves that hold only bulk canned goods can be sloped forward so that cans will roll to the front—saving you the trouble of digging for buried cans. Fasten 1-by-2 strips across the front and sides of the shelves to form channels that keep cans aligned, as shown above. Make the channels ⅛ inch wider than the height of the cans you're storing and, if possible, leave the back of the shelves accessible for loading. The shelves should slope ¾ inch for every 12 inches of shelf depth.

RECYCLING BINS Recycling bins are now commonly kept in kitchen cabinets, but if you don't have space in your kitchen, create a recycling station in your garage. The containers should be easily accessible so that you can toss material in them, and lightweight enough to carry out to the curb on collection day.

Keep bins in a well-ventilated area, since even rinsed-out cans and bottles can have an odor. Alternatively, many communities now collect all recyclable materials—paper, glass, plastic, and aluminum—together. In that case, you can use one large garbage can.

If you need to separate the materials, try using stackable plastic bins placed on the floor or on a shelving system (top, right). Attach casters to the bottoms of plastic bins or wooden crates to give them mobility.

(You can buy sets of wheels that simply snap on the bottoms of some recycle bins.) To keep several bins together, build a wooden crate to hold them. If you want to hide your recycling, install one or two slide-out undercounter garbage pails inside the bottom of a wall cabinet with doors.

HANGING RECYCLING BINS

If you have the wall space, hang plastic recycling bins one above the other on sets of angle iron brackets, cut to length and reinforced with diagonal braces bolted in place. The bins should slide in and out of the assembly easily. Keep in mind that the bins will be heavy when full, so only hang them this way from a solid wall such as one made of plywood or masonry, or use bins whose width corresponds to the spacing of the studs.

SPORTING EQUIPMENT

Sporting equipment should be stored so that it can be easily reached. A manufactured garage wall rack system can be outfitted with baskets and hooks to hold almost any kind of equipment, but with a little ingenuity and enough wall or ceiling space, you can build your own. Pegboard secured to the wall or metal shelving on tracks is a convenient place to hang lightweight sporting equipment, such as tennis rackets and bike helmets, from rubberized S-shaped hooks (right).

BALLS A wooden bin, a tall wire basket, or an open cardboard box keeps inflated basketballs and soccer balls under control in the garage. Where floor space is limited, store balls in a laundry bag hanging from a hook on the wall (below) or in a lightweight wire basket hung from a pegboard. Store balls for children at their shoulder height or lower.

GOLF EQUIPMENT Keep your golf bags off the floor and your golf shoes nearby on a wall-hanging rack (above). If you don't play frequently, store the bag in a cabinet or overhead in a storage loft.

TENNIS GEAR Hang rackets on hooks and store accessories on shelves (above). If you hang rackets on pegs, place two pegs a neck width apart and rest the racket's face on top of them.

BICYCLES   One of the hardest items to accommodate is a bicycle, especially if you have more than one. Manufactured bike racks include wall-hanging and stand-alone types, as well as floor-to-ceiling poles. There is even a ceiling rack that includes a pulley system for easy raising and lowering (above). For very little money, though, you can create a wall rack on which multiple bikes hang vertically, using a 2-by-4 runner and rubberized J-shaped hooks.

HORIZONTAL BIKE HANGER

To hang a single bike, nail two closet rod brackets side by side into the wall studs so that the half-round notches hold the bike's crossbar.

SPECIALTY RACKS   You can purchase a specialty rack to hold odd-sized sporting equipment, such as hockey sticks and kayak oars. If you have fishing gear, hang poles along the wall with S-shaped hooks or in a rod rack (above), or suspend them horizontally from the ceiling. A tackle box is best kept on a shelf.

SNOW AND WATER EQUIPMENT

Use L-shaped hooks on pegboard or attached to the wall for storing snowboards, wakeboards, and surfboards (below).

A manufactured ski rack will hold skis, poles, and boots all in one place (below, right). If you don't have the wall space, store skis and boards vertically in a shallow cabinet or horizontally suspended from the ceiling or on a storage loft. Boots should be kept in a cloth or paper bag to keep them from gathering dust and spiders.

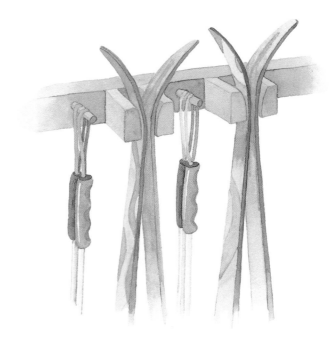

BLOCK-AND-PEG SKI RACK

With their curved tips, skis are easy to hang between blocks. Make a simple rack by fixing a pair of wood blocks to a 2-by-4 runner board for every set of skis and fastening the runner along a wall. Drill pilot holes in 2-by-4 blocks, then attach the blocks to the runner with glue and screws. Space the blocks 1¼ inch apart, rounding over and sanding their inside edges to follow the profile of the skis and prevent scratching them. Ski poles can be hung on pegs glued into holes drilled into the runner.

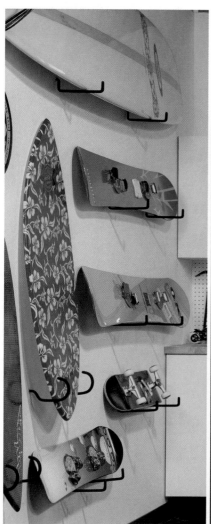

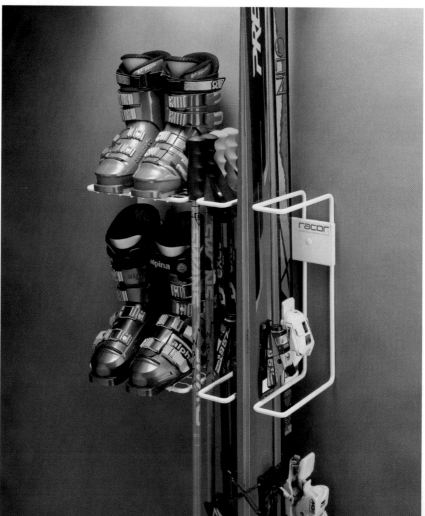

workshop

When setting up your workshop, the most important quality is accessibility. The best-equipped workshop functions poorly if items are hard to reach or disorganized. An efficient workshop also needs good light and ventilation, as well as an energy source next to the work area (top, right).

WORKBENCHES Critical to any functional workshop is a sturdy workbench. Many workbenches incorporate cabinets, drawers, hutches, and backboards (below and right). If you need a larger surface or want to create your own workbench, place a 2-foot-wide length of lumber or a flat door on top of old kitchen base cabinets or a bathroom vanity. Hang old kitchen wall cabinets above the workbench. If you don't have old cabinets, ask local contractors for discards from kitchen remodels. The cabinet drawers and shelves provide great storage for tools and accessories.

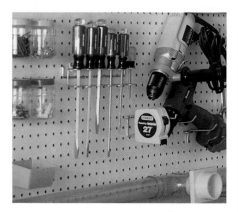

TOOL STORAGE Line the wall behind your workbench with pegboard and use it to hang hand tools from hooks (above). If it's a challenge for you to keep the board organized, you can make paper profiles of your tools and glue them to the board, providing a designated spot for each one.

Small tools or items like drill bits can be organized in a wooden or plastic utensil tray and stored on top of the workbench or in drawers in a tool chest (below). Larger tools, such as electric sanders, drills, and routers, can be stored in the same tool chest or on shelves in cabinets below the workbench.

finding a place for lumber

MOST DO-IT-YOURSELF HOME OWNERS have a few pieces of wood saved from previous jobs. If you have enough wall space, you can create horizontal storage for lumber using metal tracks with brackets (below). If your walls are exposed, use the space between the wall studs to stack lumber vertically, and secure it to the wall with wood or rubber straps.

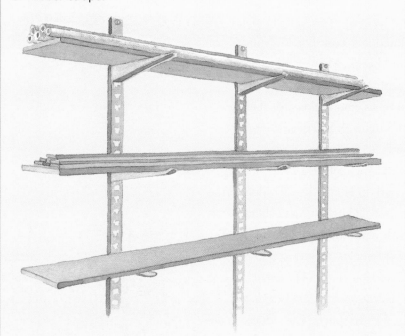

Don't forget the space up high. The area just above the top of the garage door is ideal for a long shelf. Also, if an attic or garage ceiling is left open, the space between the ceiling joists or above open rafters is ideal for storing long, thin material such as lumber or pipe (below).

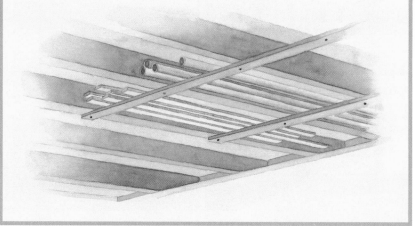

HANGING JARS UNDER A SHELF

Mounting jars under a shelf will double its storage capacity. Fasten the jar lids to the shelf with screws and washers, then screw the jars to the lids.

Finding the right-size nails can be a chore. Divide nails by size and keep them in labeled glass jars or plastic containers on shelves (below) or in drawers. If you store nails in glass jars, you can screw the lids to the underside of a shelf or cabinet and then screw the jars into the lids (left).

You can also purchase a plastic storage box with bins made specifically for hardware (below, left) or use a drawer organizer with multiple compartments to store nails and screws by size.

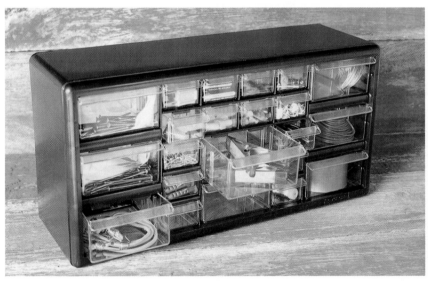

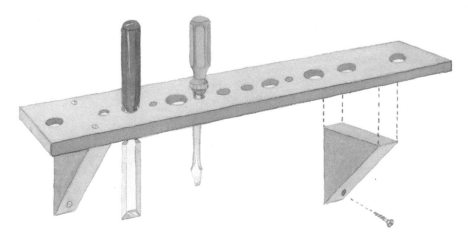

WALL-MOUNTED TOOL RACK

Drill holes through a length of 1-by-4 lumber and attach it to the wall with wooden braces to hold tools such as screwdrivers and chisels.

PROJECT: folding workbench

If you don't have much space in your garage, but you need a work surface as well as a place to store tools and fasteners, or craft materials, such as fabric, paint, and accessories, this 72-inch-long folding workbench is especially efficient. When open, it requires a 46-inch depth clearance. When closed, it projects only 8 inches from the wall. You can change the depth to suit your needs.

MATERIALS

- Five 8-ft. lengths of 1-by-6 pine board
- $1\frac{1}{2}$-in. finishing nails
- Two 8-ft. lengths of 1-by-2 pine board
- One 4-by-4-ft. sheet of $\frac{1}{8}$-in. pegboard
- 4-in. headed nails
- One 4-by-8-ft. sheet of $\frac{3}{4}$-in. plywood
- One 8-ft. length of 2-by-4 Douglas fir board
- No. 8 flathead wood screws
- Four 5-in. T-hinges
- Two 10-in. double-arm lid supports
- One latching hasp

CUTTING THE SHELVES Cut the 1-by-6 board to the following lengths for the shelves: two pieces, $70\frac{1}{2}$ inches; two pieces, $37\frac{1}{2}$ inches; one piece, $36\frac{3}{4}$ inches; four pieces, 36 inches; four pieces, 6 inches.

CREATING THE BOX Butt-joint the two $37\frac{1}{2}$-inch boards onto the two $70\frac{1}{2}$-inch boards to create a rectangular box with outside dimensions of $37\frac{1}{2}$ by 72 inches. Nail the boards together with $1\frac{1}{2}$-inch finishing nails. Nail one 6-inch board into the center of one 36-inch shelf board, and set this into the box so that the long board butts into a short side of the box and the 6-inch board butts into a long side of the box. Nail through the outside of the box into the edges of both boards.

Next, set the $36\frac{3}{4}$-inch board in the box on end and butt it up against the 36-inch shelf. Nail

above the floor. Draw a level line along these marks. Mark the locations of studs just above this line as well as 40 inches above it. Position the top of the second furring strip along the line and nail it into the studs, using 4-inch headed nails **(B)**. Rest the bottom of the box on top of the furring strip, place it against the wall, and nail the top furring strip into studs **(C)**. Nail the box to the lower furring strip.

ATTACHING THE LEGS TO THE TABLETOP

Cut two pieces of the 2-by-4 to 36 inches for the legs. Mount them to one side of the 4-by-8-foot sheet of $\frac{3}{4}$-inch plywood (the tabletop work surface), 8 inches in from both sides and 2 inches in from the front, with the T-hinges. Secure them with no. 8 flathead wood screws.

Mount the lid supports (used to hold the legs at a 90-degree angle when the tabletop is open) 7 inches from the top of the legs and $\frac{3}{8}$ inch in from the outside, back edges of the legs. Screw the other two T-hinges to the top, back edge of the tabletop, 8 inches in from the sides.

ATTACHING THE TABLETOP

Butt the plywood tabletop up to the bottom edge of the box and attach the T-hinges to the bottom shelf **(D)**. Attach the latching hasp to the underside of the table and to the frame at the top, to hold the table vertically when not in use.

through the outside of the box into this center divider.

Stand the box frame up on a flat surface, and repeat the process of nailing the 6-inch boards into the 36-inch shelves and installing them in the left side of the box until you have four shelves in place **(A)**. Next, nail the sheet of pegboard to the back of the right side of the box.

ATTACHING THE BOX TO THE WALL

Mark the wall in several places approximately $35\frac{1}{4}$ inches

Cut two 72-inch-long furring strips from the 1-by-2 pine. Nail one of them to the back top of the box frame so that the bottom of the strip is flush with the back top edge of the frame board. The strip will extend above the frame by $\frac{3}{4}$ inch.

seasonal and long-term storage

Items you don't use frequently or are saving for a rainy day can be stored out of normal reach—either high on shelves, suspended from the ceiling, or under the basement stairs. However, you should still be able to locate and access them easily. Anything stored long term should be labeled and protected in bags or containers against moisture, dust, rodents, and insects.

HOLIDAY DECORATIONS How often have you purchased new decorations because you forgot where you stored the ones from the year before? The best way to organize them is to put them in labeled plastic or cardboard boxes—a different one for each holiday you celebrate. The toughest things to store safely are holiday tree ornaments and lights, and blown eggs.

You can store ornaments in their original boxes or in specialty ornament boxes with individual compartments that protect them from breakage (top, right). Keep lights untangled by wrapping them around a large sheet of cardboard notched with Vs or a large cardboard tube, and store them in a flat plastic box (above). The following year you can unroll the lights from the board or tube as you walk around the tree. Blown eggs can be placed in cardboard egg boxes. Wrap items such as menorahs, statues, and holiday serving pieces in cotton sheeting, old towels, or tissue paper and place them in boxes. Then stack the boxes on shelves (right) or in labeled trunks or bins.

CAMPING EQUIPMENT Most camping equipment, such as tents, sleeping bags, stoves, collapsible chairs, and coolers, stacks easily and is light enough to store up high. Keep it on the upper shelves of cabinets or a wall system. Manufactured wire shelves can be suspended from a high ceiling (left). Or create a loft shelf, either suspended from the ceiling joists or tucked above open rafters.

overhead storage

MANY GARAGES AND ATTICS have high or open ceilings that provide a place for extra storage, either suspended from the joists or built between the joists and rafters. Since you may need a ladder to access this area, you should only store things here that are used infrequently and are light enough to lift down easily. Empty suitcases, lightweight camping gear, seasonal sporting equipment, and cushions from patio furniture can all be stored overhead.

In a garage or attic that is open between the joists and rafters, straddle items on the rafters or set sheets of plywood on top of the rafters to create overhead shelving.

If the space has a flat ceiling, you can build in suspended shelving using 2-by-4 stock and plywood (right). Assemble two or more sets of wooden racks with lag screws or bolts, making sure they are wide enough to support a shelf (3 feet is a good distance). The length of the verticals depends on the height of your ceiling and the amount of clearance you need. Bolt the uprights of each rack to a joist. Racks should be no more than 4 feet apart. Nail a sheet of plywood on top of two or more racks to create the shelf.

SPACE ABOVE JOISTS
In many garages there is usable storage space between the joists or collar beams overhead and the rafters. This space provides a ready-to-use storage place for your seasonal items.

SUSPENDED SHELVES
U-shaped racks made from 2-by-4 stock and attached to ceiling joists are handy for long-term storage.

CLOTHING   Used children's clothing or out-of-season outfits often make their way to the attic or basement. If you store clothing in fabric garment bags, be sure to hang them on wooden hangers rather than wire ones. Hang garment bags from closet rods that are fastened between the rafters in an attic, or from furring strips screwed across the ceiling joists in a basement or insulated garage. (Never bore holes through joists for the rods.) You can also set up a collapsible hanging rod in an unused corner (right).

The ideal solution is to line a freestanding or built-in wardrobe with cedar and store hanging bags inside. Folded clothes should be wrapped in tissue before being placed in cedar-lined trunks or boxes. Clothing should always be clean and stored in a dry area—excessive dampness creates mold.

QUILTS, BLANKETS, AND LINENS
Fold or roll linens, and wrap them in clean cotton pillowcases or sheets or in layers of tissue paper—never in plastic. Then store them overhead or in trunks (left). Quilts and linens should be taken out of their cases and refolded at least once a year to prevent creases from discoloring. Woolen blankets should be preserved with mothballs or stored in cedar chests.

DOCUMENT STORAGE By law you are required to save your tax records for at least three years after you file your taxes. Keep them in cardboard document boxes (left). Property and other investment records need to be held indefinitely. The best way to do this is to store your records in file folders and keep them in acid- and lignin-free document boxes. The boxes can be stacked high on shelves or above the rafters. If you have sufficient floor space, you can also store records in old vertical file cabinets you can buy cheaply at a used-office-furniture store or a garage sale.

firewood

THE GARAGE IS A GOOD PLACE to shelter firewood from the elements. But keeping it contained can be a challenge. Whether your wood is dry and seasoned or recently cut, it must be kept from ground moisture and stored so that air can circulate around it. Wood can be stacked in either parallel or perpendicular (crisscross) rows. Store a pile of wood under the basement stairs off the floor or in an open cabinet in the garage. Metal firewood holders with side supports also hold a good supply of wood indoors.

Firewood can become infested with anything from ants to wood beetles. Minimize or prevent this problem by keeping the wood off the ground. Never store wood up against the outside of your house, as insects can make their way inside through cracks in the foundation. (If you're storing wood outside, keep it at least 10 feet from the wall, if possible.) Bang the wood against the ground to dislodge as many insects as possible before you bring it inside.

To reduce the risk of insects' spreading in the house, only bring in wood as you need it; in general, don't store more than a few days' worth of wood inside. As an additional precaution, you can surround the inside firewood bin with sticky glue strips to catch any insects that wander away from the woodpile. Glue strips are more effective than bait traps, which actually attract certain kinds of insects.

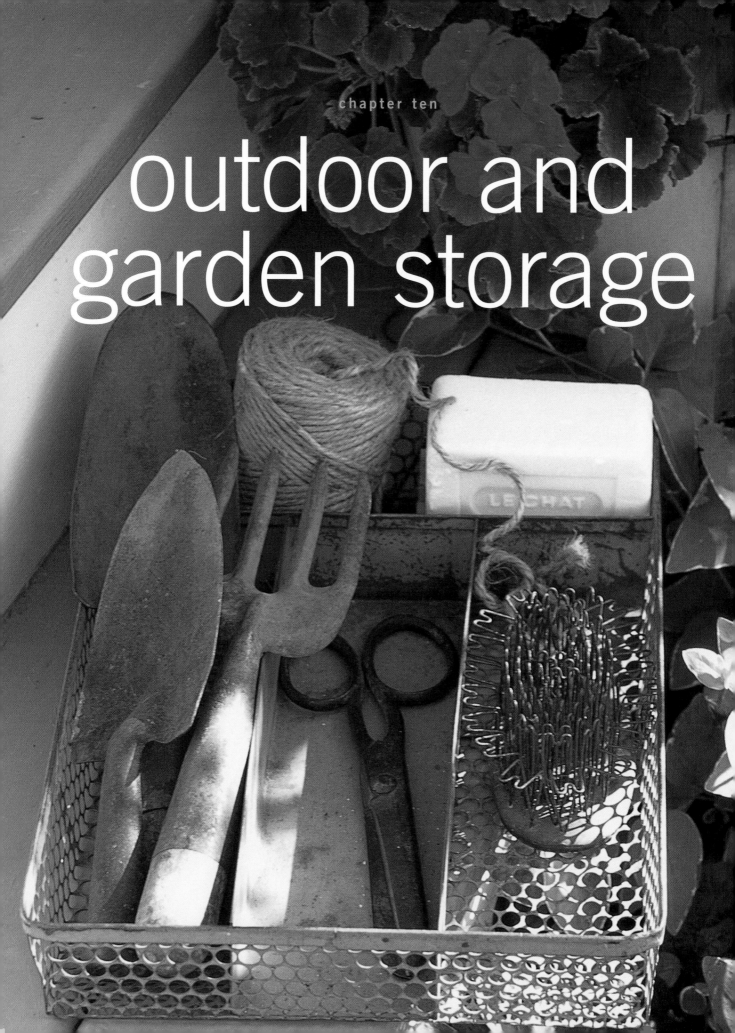

outdoor and garden storage

PICTURE-PERFECT GARDENS MAY LOOK almost effortless, but gardening aficionados know that keeping grass green and flowers in bloom takes work. Outdoor living is easier when furniture, tools, and supplies are right at hand as needed. Surprisingly, enthusiasts claim to enjoy the labor involved in their pastime as much as the rewards. Your deck, patio, and outdoor areas can blossom, too, once you determine how and where to store the items you regularly use there.

Adding a garden shed allows you to organize and store seasonal supplies, as well as room to tend plants. You may even squeeze out space in which to stash patio furniture and barbecue gear. Don't despair if your yard lacks room for a shed; consider a tool hutch, a potting bench, or a storage box that hides under the deck. This chapter offers ideas for a variety of containers and structures to help you round up and efficiently stow your outdoor items.

deck and patio

Life is good when you're sitting outside overlooking a beautiful garden with a cool drink in your hand and a meal sizzling on the grill. So don't let cluttered space mar the moment. Finding sensible storage sites helps you clear the deck or patio and prepare for each season. Collect outdoor dishes, garden tools, and other supplies in a storage closet (right), and move anything you're not using regularly to a storage area under or near your deck (below, right).

STORAGE BOX A large storage box is a good place to keep cushions, game equipment, outdoor table-cloths, and other patio items when not in use so that they're within easy reach yet out of the elements (below). You can buy large wooden or plastic boxes with wheels on one side and a swivel handle that make them easy to move. Pick a box with a padded top if you need extra seating. If you build a box, hinge the top and make it sturdy enough to use as a seat with waterproof cushions.

OUTDOOR FURNITURE Patio and deck furniture should be not only comfortable and durable but also easy to cover or haul into storage when winter approaches. Buy folding versions of chairs, tables, and lounges for off-season storage, and choose heavy-duty, weatherproof models made from materials such as teak, redwood, metal, or plastic for year-round use.

To save storage space, hang lightweight folding chairs and recliners under the eaves or in a shed from wall studs on long nails or wood dowels (far right). Shelf brackets or L-braces will also work (near right). Furniture can be stored in a garden shed, a shallow cabinet under the eaves of the house, or even the garage, if you have space.

GRILLS AND SUPPLIES If you use a grill only occasionally, look for one on wheels that you can move easily in and out of storage, or select a small, portable grill to save off-season storage space. Keep charcoal in a plastic garbage can or storage box nearby (below). Stow supplies you don't use at least weekly, grouping like items: grill equipment and supplies; outdoor tableware; citronella candles, insecticides, and insect repellants; furniture and accessories.

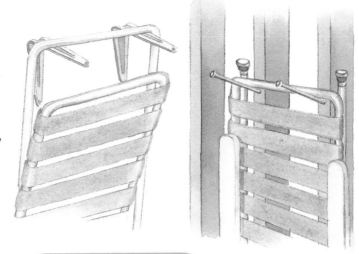

below the deck

THE UNUSED SPACE BELOW THE SURFACE of most decks is ideal for building a storage compartment for garden tools or a small barbecue in the off-season. To install a trap door, cut the decking so that the ends of the door rest on the center of a joist or beam. Build a container and attach it to the underside of the deck. Drill a hole in the bottom for drainage.

On the door's underside, fasten 1-by-3 battens offset from the ends and parallel to the joists or beams to keep the door securely seated. Add a third batten diagonally between the first two. Install a recessed pull on the door. You can simply set the door in place and lift it out as necessary, or use butt hinges to fasten one end to the deck.

garden gear

Good tools are expensive and deserve good maintenance. If garden implements are cleaned after each use and stored in a dry place, they will continue to give service year after year. For easy access, store tools close to your working area. Add portable storage, too, such as a rolling hose trolley, to keep necessities close at hand. Or carry small tools with you in a basket, tray, or box with handles.

HAND TOOLS Containers with places for small tools and other garden implements are handy for tending plants. Some gardeners prefer to tie on specially designed aprons with pockets for gloves and tools. These hands-free aprons are available at home and garden centers. You can also buy a canvas satchel that wraps around a bucket and holds hand tools (top, right). A rolling tool organizer with wire grids holds tall, thin tools. It glides easily around the garden on casters or locks into place for shed storage.

HANGING TOOLS One of the best ways to store garden tools is to group them by type and hang them up so they're easy to retrieve when needed. Lining a wall with pegboard creates a practical and inexpensive backdrop for storing tools (left). Tall, thin items such as rakes, edgers, shovels, and hoes can be hung on a wall-mounted rack from hooks, pegs (above), or special holders that grasp the handle with rollers. Place tools with the heads up rather than down to keep them away from children, and stow pruners and other sharp tools well out of reach.

TOOL STASH   If your garden is limited to container plantings on the patio or deck, you still need a place to store tools, pots, and supplies. Nailing up a board and adding pegs or hooks organizes small tools and watering cans. Attaching a small cupboard, painted or stained to withstand moisture, to a spare section of wall is another solution. If you have an old rake, mount it on an outside wall and hang your frequently used tools from its tines (below).

HOSE HOW-TO   No matter how carefully garden hoses are coiled, they always seem to tangle or kink in storage. A commercial hose coiler prevents this by keeping the hose firmly wrapped around a drum. The hose reels off the drum when pulled out for use and recoils when the handle is turned the other way. Stationary reels attach to the house near the spigot; reels on wheels (top) can be moved to a spigot and returned to storage when watering is done. A terra-cotta or clay pot will also keep a hose both coiled and concealed (above).

storing tools and supplies safely

TO KEEP YOUR HAND TOOLS IN GOOD SHAPE, use a bucket of sand to clean them before storing them for the season. Simply push the tool up and down in the sand a few times before you put it away. If you wash off dirt, dry the tool carefully to keep it from rusting. In damp areas, treat tools with liquid rust cleaner, emery paper, or a wire brush after cleaning; oil metal surfaces before storing.

Moisture damages potting soils, fertilizers, and plant food, so store these bags inside sealed plastic containers or in covered and labeled trash cans with tight-fitting lids. Use metal containers to keep rodents and insects out of grass seed and bird feed. Garden poisons and sprayers need to be kept in locked cabinets to prevent accidents from happening to curious children and family pets.

small work centers

You may dream about a true garden shed—a separate structure that also has space to pot plants. But if you don't have enough room for a shed, think smaller. How about adding a potting bench, a potting alcove (right), or a skinny tool closet? With organization, even a small area can accommodate tools, pots, fertilizers, and other garden supplies.

POTTING BENCHES One invaluable item for any garden is a good potting bench. It has a work surface for tending plants (below) and contains space you can use to organize garden gear. If your potting bench has cabinets below, store pots, watering cans, soil, fertilizers, and other supplies behind its doors (right). Add a garbage can for debris and old pots or baskets to organize plant labels, scissors, twine, and other necessities.

During the gardening season, stack clean, dry pots outside on or near your potting bench. During winter, tuck them inside each other, lay the stacks on their sides, and store them in a shed or garage to ensure that they won't break if your area is one that experiences freezing temperatures.

folding potting center

A FREESTANDING POTTING CENTER is basically a large cabinet with shelves, dividers, doors, and a fold-down work surface—all made from ¾-inch exterior-grade plywood with a weatherproof finish. Use butt hinges to attach the work surface to the cabinet. Add a single leg with a butt hinge and folding leg braces for support. Fasten hasps (door fasteners with a hinged metal strap that fits over a staple) to the cabinet to hold the work surface in place when it's folded up. If you store soil or amendments inside the bottom of the cabinet, drill ventilation holes into the sides.

Metal garbage cans are ideal for storing peat moss, soil, and fertilizer. You can build a simple rack that fits inside the cabinet and holds the cans at an angle for easy access.

SUPPLY HIDEOUTS A wooden storage closet in the garden serves as a way station between the house and the far corners of the garden (above). Reach inside for pots, gloves, and small tools; return items on your way indoors. A wooden structure must withstand the elements, so rot-resistant wood—cypress, cedar, redwood, or teak—and galvanized hinges and screws are important. Any wood but teak needs marine varnish or exterior stain.

PROJECT: garden shed

If you are tired of lugging tools in and out of a cluttered garage or searching endlessly for lost ones, the perfect solution is to house them in this handsome storage shed. Easy to build, the good-sized tool shed provides space—and protection—for all your garden tools. Racks offer stand-up space for long-handled shovels, spades, rakes, and hoes, as well as floor room for shorter tools, hoses, and watering cans. Stand the shed against the side of the house, in the back of the patio or deck, or along a fence in the garden. If the shed is placed on the ground, mount it on bricks or stepping-stones to protect the floor from rot.

MATERIALS

- Four 8-ft. lengths of 2-by-4 Douglas fir board
- 3-in. box nails
- Three 4-by-8-ft. pieces of ⅜-in. siding
- 1¼-in. galvanized nails
- Two 8-ft. lengths of 1-by-12 pine scrap lumber
- Four 6-in. T-hinges
- One 4½-in. latching hasp
- One roll of roof edging

MAKING THE UPPER AND LOWER FRAMES From the 2-by-4 boards, cut four pieces 35½ inches long and four pieces 14¾ inches long. Nail the pieces together to form two 35½-by-17¾-inch frames, using 3-inch box nails (A).

CUTTING THE SIDING Lay out the cuts that will be made from the siding so that you can get all the sections from the three sheets. Cut the siding into the following parts: two 18-by-72-inch pieces for the sides; one 22-by-41-inch piece for the roof (can be made of two or more parts); one 17-by-35½-inch piece for the base (can be made of two or more parts); two 2-by-66-inch pieces for the side trim; two 3-by-32-inch pieces for the bottom and top trim; two 16¼-by-61-inch pieces for the doors; one 36-by-72-inch piece for the back.

back. Using the drilled holes as reference, cut out three slots on each piece (B).

Cut four $^3/_4$-by-2-by-10-inch boards from any scrap lumber. Nail them to both sides at 24 and 48 inches from the bottom to act as ledger strips for the tool rack (for more information on ledger strips, see page 185).

Set the bottom of the tool rack on top of the ledger strips and nail in place. Now nail the two 24-inch boards vertically to the 35$^1/_2$-inch part of the rack you just nailed into place, 12 inches in from each end. Place the second 35$^1/_2$-inch board on the top ledger strips and the 24-inch vertical support boards and nail into place.

ADDING THE DOORS AND ROOF

Install the doors using the T-hinges, and place a small piece of scrap siding behind each hinge and latch to accept the nail ends and prevent them from sticking out into the cabinet (C). Attach the two 3-by-32-inch pieces for the bottom and top trim to the frame above and below the doors. Nail the roof in place and cover it with edging material (D).

Cut off the tops of the sides at 80 degrees, turning one sheet over before you cut so that the siding will face out on both sides. Nail the sides and back to the upper and lower frames using 1$^1/_4$-inch galvanized nails.

PREPARING THE INTERIOR TOOL RACK From the 12-inch-wide pine board, cut two pieces 35$^1/_2$ inches long and four pieces 24 inches long. On the two 35$^1/_2$-inch boards, drill 2-inch-diameter holes at 9, 17$^3/_4$, and 26$^1/_2$ inches, 2 inches from the

garden sheds and recycling areas

Storage sheds come in all shapes and sizes, from small plastic or metal models to custom wooden structures (right). Choose a shed that matches your needs and the style of your house and garden. Don't overlook the possibility of building a covered area for garbage cans and recycling bins. An open, shedlike structure will keep the trash zone tidy and sheltered from the elements.

SELECTING A SITE

On a large rural lot, there are rarely restrictions on the placement or style of shed you choose. But in most cities, you need to check into guidelines about easements, set-backs, and height and lot coverage limits. Keep in mind that sheds exceeding 100 square feet might be subject to building code regulations and require a permit. It's wise to take measurements and a sketch of your shed to the local planning department to see if code or zoning requirements apply.

GARDEN SHEDS Any storage shed benefits from certain elements—plenty of hanging space for tools, a work surface, and a safe spot to keep sharp implements and harmful chemicals away from children and pets. If a shed is used for working with plants, it also needs shelves and cabinets for supplies and pots (right), and ideally it has a sink or a nearby water source.

EQUIPMENT SHEDS Large equipment needs plenty of storage space and a clear path to the outdoors. Shed doors should be wide enough and have sills low enough for easy passage of large seasonal equipment unblocked (right)—lawn mowers in summer, mulchers in fall. A smaller shed keeps recreational gear properly stored but within easy reach (below).

TALKING TRASH Trash cans are a not-so-attractive necessity of most houses. They are usually open to the elements or tucked under the overhang of the house or garage between pickups. Keep cans in a covered structure to block your view of them (below, left), or hide them behind a small trellis or decorative fence. Plant a fast-growing vine or evergreen shrub near the trellis, fence, or structure to add to the camouflage.

If your area doesn't supply a separate container for disposing of lawn and garden trimmings, buy a can with wheels for yard cleanup. This type of can requires less labor and accumulates less wear and tear on its glide to the curb—a real advantage when it's fully loaded with grass clippings.

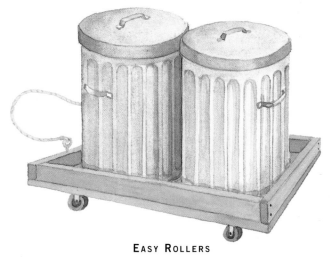

EASY ROLLERS

Don't lug heavy garbage cans to the curb and back. Simplify pick-up day by mounting trash cans on a wagon. From ⅝-inch plywood cut a base large enough to hold two cans. To make the lip, attach a frame of 2-by-4s around the perimeter. Fasten heavy-duty casters to the underside of the base at each corner, and thread a cord through two bolts to form a handle.

tools and techniques

Whether you are assembling a manufactured storage system or construct-ing a custom unit yourself, you need certain building skills. Prefabricated systems are relatively easy to assemble with limited tools and experience. Custom-building, however, requires a greater variety of tools as well as some knowledge of woodworking.

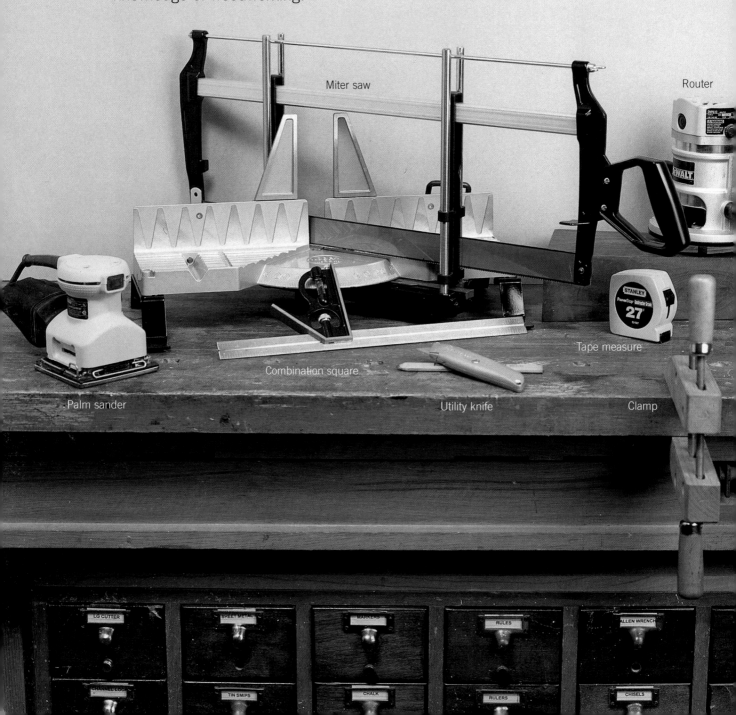

Miter saw

Router

Tape measure

Combination square

Utility knife

Palm sander

Clamp

In this chapter, you will learn what skills are needed to complete the eight projects in this book, as well as techniques required to build simple storage cubes, bookcases, and shelving. You will also learn the most secure ways to fasten heavy storage units to the wall—an important issue if you live in an area prone to earthquakes.

THE RIGHT TOOLS

Before you begin any job, you should have on hand the tools and fasteners you need to do the job right. Some of the tools you are most likely to use to install or build a storage unit are displayed on these pages. If you are new to building, stock your workshop with the basic hand tools shown here—of the best quality you can afford—and then purchase more specialized power tools as you need them. If you require an expensive tool for

Carpenter's glue
Cordless drill
Screwdriver
Finishing nails
European-style hinges
Screws
Hammer
Toggle bolts

a specific project, you can rent almost anything on an hourly or daily basis from a tool-rental business in your area.

Fasteners such as nails and screws are basic to any building project. Nails are easiest to use, screws provide more strength, and bolts with nuts are even stronger. But the strongest fastener for a wood joint is a good adhesive, such as carpenter's glue. (In some cases, you need to hold a joint together with nails until the glue is dry.)

Before you use any power tool, be sure to read the owner's manual carefully and follow the suggested safety precautions, such as wearing work gloves, safety goggles, and earplugs, as appropriate. Use a respirator when applying paints or toxic adhesives and a dust mask when sanding or sawing.

Table saw

fastening to walls

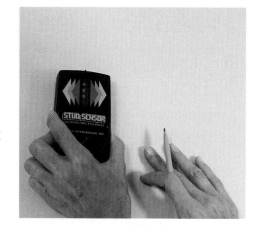

Message boards and heavy storage pieces such as bookcases and cabinets should be fastened securely to a wall to prevent them from falling due to an imbalanced load or an earthquake. In a wood-framed house, fasten furniture to the wall or ceiling framing (studs, top plates, or joists) with nails or screws.

If you have to fasten something into hollow drywall, plaster, or solid masonry, or you're attaching something that won't hold much weight, such as a wooden key rack, you can use specialty fasteners to ensure a secure attachment. Many closet-organizer systems come with their own versions of plastic anchor bolts for this purpose.

FASTENING TO WALL STUDS
Studs, the vertical boards that frame a wall, and ceiling joists, the framing that holds up the ceiling, are usually spaced 16 to 24 inches apart on center (from center to center). The easiest way to locate them is to use an electronic or magnetic stud finder (top, right). You can also find studs or joists by knocking on the wall with the heel of your hand. A solid sound signifies a stud, and a hollow sound indicates the space between. If this doesn't work, drill small exploratory holes in the wall or ceiling until you hit wood. Once you've found the stud or ceiling joist, use drywall screws to attach your storage unit to the wall or ceiling.

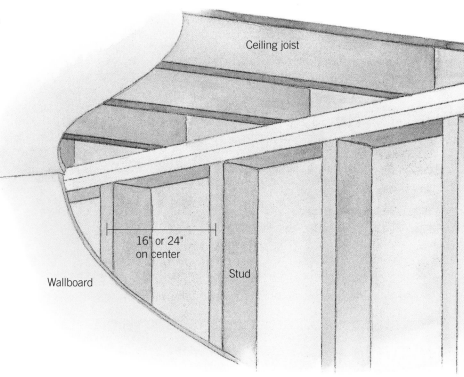

Ceiling joist

16" or 24" on center

Wallboard

Stud

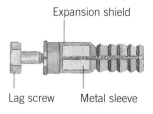

Expansion shield

Lag screw   Metal sleeve

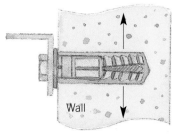

Wall

FASTENING TO MASONRY Use an expansion shield when attaching anything to a brick or concrete wall. Drill a hole into the wall as wide as the sleeve but slightly longer. Insert the sleeve into the hole and then tap it in place with your hammer. Insert a lag screw through the part of the storage unit to be fastened and into the sleeve. The anchor will expand as the screw is tightened.

FASTENING INTO WALLBOARD OR PLASTER Often it is necessary to attach a storage unit to the wall between the wall studs. In this case you need to use a spreading anchor or toggle bolt that has wings or a sleeve that opens against the back of the finish wall to hold the fastener securely in place. Install spreading anchors and toggle bolts according to package instructions.

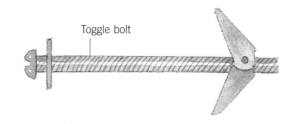
Toggle bolt

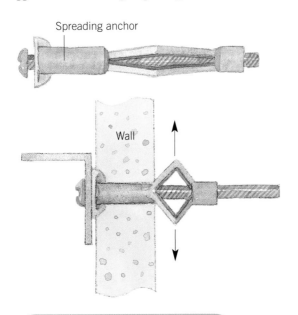
Spreading anchor

Wall

Wall

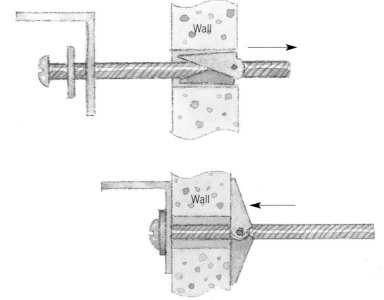
Wall

Wall

installing pegboard

THE SECRET TO INSTALLING pegboard (perforated hardboard) is to make sure there is a space between it and the wall so the pegs or hooks can fit through the holes. You can fasten narrow strips of wood (furring strips) to the wall, into studs, and attach the pegboard to these strips. The simplest way to create this space, though, is to slip a spacer over the screw before threading it into the anchor or toggle. The spacer holds the board out from the wall.

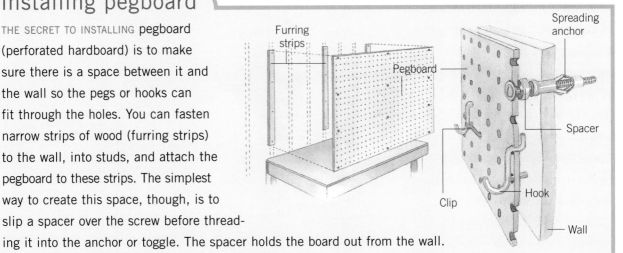
Furring strips
Pegboard
Spreading anchor
Spacer
Hook
Clip
Wall

One classic problem with pegboard is keeping hooks in place. Look for hooks with an anti-pullout design. If you can't find any, a good trick is to use small plastic clips, available at hardware stores, that fit over the hooks and lock them to the holes on each side. The clips can be pried off with a pocketknife if you wish to move the hooks.

basic joinery

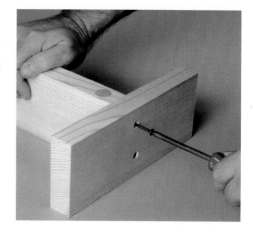

The way in which wood furniture is joined together at the corners affects both its appearance and its strength. There are many ways to make joints; the joinery you will use to construct simple cubes, bookcases, and other projects in this book includes butt, lap, dado, and rabbet joints. If you have never done any finish carpentry, experiment with scraps of wood before you begin building.

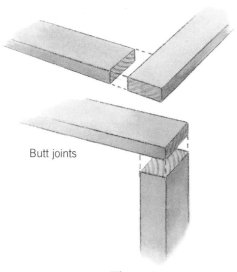

Butt joints

BUTT JOINT The easiest joinery method is a "butt joint," in which the face or edge of one board is attached to the face, edge, or end of another. A butt joint is used when appearance and strength aren't critical. Edge-to-edge butt joints can be glued together for a tight bond; clamp the pieces together while the glue dries. End grains (cut edges perpendicular rather than parallel to the grain) will not hold together with glue alone. When joining an end grain to any other side of a board, glue and then use nails or screws to strengthen the joint. The nail or screw should be twice as long as the thickness of the piece it is passing through.

LAP JOINT Used to join the faces of two boards that meet at right angles, "lap joints" are formed by cutting a recess across the grain of one or both of the boards. When one board is thicker than another and a recess is cut in only the thicker board, the joint is called a "full-lap joint." When the recess is cut in both boards, it is called a "half-lap joint." A lap joint is very strong and will hold together with glue alone.

DADO JOINT A notch cut across the face of a board to fit the plain edge of another board is called a "dado." A dado can be cut up to two-thirds the thickness of the board. Generally a dado joint is secured with glue along with nails or screws. A dado is much stronger than a butt joint and is often used to join a shelf or vertical partition to the inside of a case.

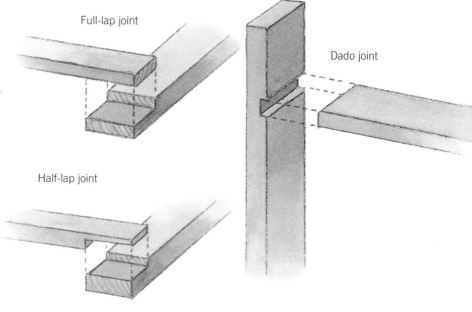

Full-lap joint

Half-lap joint

Dado joint

RABBET JOINT Similar to a dado, a "rabbet" is a notch at the end of the board. Rabbet joints are often used on the outside corners of cases to give them more stability.

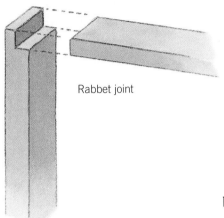

Rabbet joint

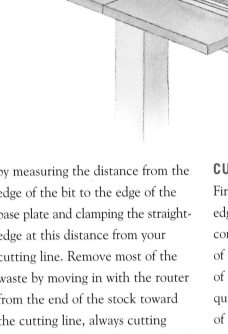

First cut

Cutting line

CUTTING A LAP JOINT WITH A ROUTER

To make a wide recess for a lap joint, first mark the inside edge of the recess. Clamp the stock to your workbench, adding a scrap piece along each edge to prevent the edges from splintering.

Adjust the router so the depth of the cut is exactly half the stock's thickness. Set a straightedge guide by measuring the distance from the edge of the bit to the edge of the base plate and clamping the straightedge at this distance from your cutting line. Remove most of the waste by moving in with the router from the end of the stock toward the cutting line, always cutting against the rotation of the router bit. Then make a final pass, using the straightedge as a guide. Smooth the bottom of the recess with a chisel or block plane.

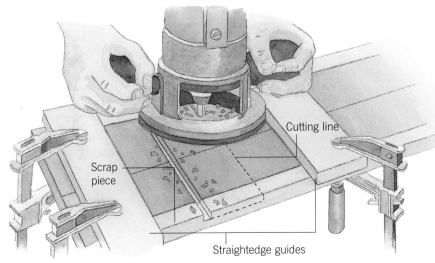

Scrap piece

Cutting line

Straightedge guides

CUTTING A DADO OR RABBET

First, measure and mark the outside edges of the wood. Then set a combination square for the depth of the recess and mark the bottom of the cut. The cut should be one-quarter to one-third the thickness of the board. To make the cut, use a circular saw or router.

The thickness of plywood differs slightly from one manufacturer and grade to another. For example, $\frac{3}{4}$-inch plywood is now cut about $\frac{1}{32}$ inch narrower than it once was and will float in a $\frac{3}{4}$-inch dado. Instead of cutting a $\frac{3}{4}$-inch dado, cut a $\frac{1}{4}$-inch dado in the receiving board and a $\frac{1}{4}$-inch rabbet in the end of the plywood, or start with a $\frac{1}{4}$-inch dado and build the groove to fit the plywood. If you're cutting dadoes to attach shelves to a case, clamp together the sides of the case and make the cuts in both sides at once to ensure that they line up correctly.

boxes and cases

A simple box or case is easy to make and offers a versatile storage solution. Boxes and cases follow the same construction principles, using five basic pieces—two sides, a back, a top, and a bottom. Shelves can be added as needed.

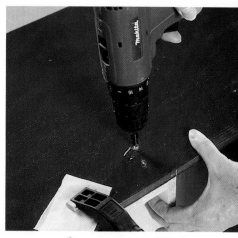

CHOOSING A JOINT

Butt joints are probably the commonest and easiest type of joinery for separate pieces of wood. To make a strong box with butt joints, have the top overlap the sides and the bottom butt into the sides (below). If you are using 1-by lumber, the top needs to be $1\frac{1}{2}$ inches wider than the bottom. The sides will be the same size. Square or rectangular boxes can be stacked together to create an attractive wall storage system. For extra support and safety, bolt high stacks of boxes together or to a wall.

For a much more durable bookcase, attach the top to the sides with rabbet joints and the bottom to the sides with dado joints (right). You will need to cut a rabbet in both ends of your top piece. If you want a kick space at the bottom of your box or case, cut the dadoes several inches from the bottom edges of the sides.

Before you assemble the five pieces, plan the order in which you will put together the case. The assembly is affected by the way you attach any shelves. If you are building a case without shelves, first reinforce the joints by putting glue in the dadoes and attaching the two sides to the bottom. Then glue the top to the sides and add nails or screws to secure the joints. Finally, attach the back. A $\frac{1}{4}$-inch-plywood back will hold the unit square.

Basic case

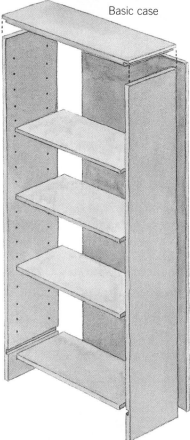

Standard box

actual measurements of lumber

AT HOME-IMPROVEMENT centers	NOMINAL	ACTUAL
and lumberyards, boards are	1-by-1	$\frac{3}{4}$ by $\frac{3}{4}$ inches
cut smaller than their names	1-by-2	$\frac{3}{4}$ by $1\frac{1}{2}$ inches
imply unless they are specially	1-by-4	$\frac{3}{4}$ by $3\frac{1}{2}$ inches
milled. With any woodworking	2-by-4	$1\frac{1}{2}$ by $3\frac{1}{2}$ inches
project, measure twice and cut	2-by-6	$1\frac{1}{2}$ by $5\frac{1}{2}$ inches
once to save time and money.	4-by-6	$3\frac{1}{2}$ by $5\frac{1}{2}$ inches

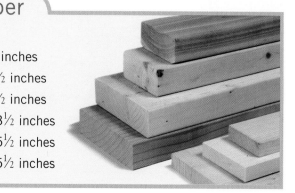

SHELVING OPTIONS

Shelves can be made of the same wood used to make the case. You can also make them of plywood, particleboard, or MDF (medium-density fiberboard) with or without a laminate covering. The front edges of the shelves can be left plain, edged with wood, molded, or faced with a wood frame.

There are several ways to attach shelves to your case, including the use of ledgers, dadoes, and clips. Ledgers and dadoes are fixed, while clips let you adjust the height of your shelves. If your case is rectangular, you should have at least one fixed shelf approximately halfway between the top and bottom for strength.

LEDGERS The simplest way to attach shelves is to nail ledger strips along the inner sides and back of the finished case and then set the shelves on top of them. The advantage of ledgers is that they provide support to the entire length of the shelf. If appearance is an issue, you can rout the visible edges of the ledger strips for decoration.

DADOES When shelves are dadoed into the sides of the case, the entire case is made more durable. The shelves support more weight. The dadoes should be the same width as the thickness of the shelf. Before assembling the case, cut dadoes in both sides of the case at the same time so they line up. Lay one sidepiece on a worktable and spread glue in the dadoes. Tap the shelves in place, using a rubber mallet if they don't slide in easily. Fit the other side on top. Use two pipe or bar clamps for each joint to secure the assembly while the glue dries. Next, stand the case upright, glue the top edges of the sides, and fit the top board in place. Reinforce all joints with nails or screws. Attach the back.

CLIPS An almost invisible way to support adjustable shelves is to drill two vertical rows of $\frac{1}{4}$-inch holes on the inside faces of the sides of the case and insert metal or plastic L-shaped clips in the holes. The shelves are placed on the clips. The holes should be about 2 inches apart along the vertical lines and an inch from the outside edges of the sides. The easiest way to ensure that your holes are lined up is to use a plexiglass shelving jig, available through woodworking catalogs.

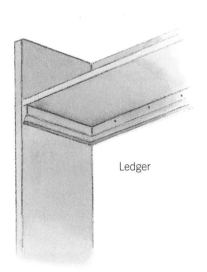

Ledger

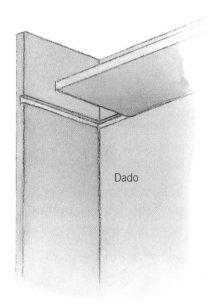

Dado

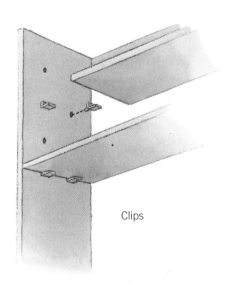

Clips

finishing touches

You can dress up a plain box or cabinet to complement the style of your home with edge treatments, face frames, and a coat of paint or stain. These finishing touches will not only enhance the appearance of your storage unit but also protect it from wear and tear. Remember to wear eye protection when routing and hammering, and use rubber gloves and a respirator, if necessary, when applying oil-based stains or paints.

EDGE TREATMENTS

If you have made the case out of plywood or MDF, you may want to cover the front edges of the case and shelves (unless you have built the case for use in a garage or attic, where appearance isn't as important). A wooden case does not require edging but will benefit from its decorative and protective qualities. There are several ways to add detail to the edges of your case and shelves. If you want a traditional look, create a decorative edge treatment along the front and sides of the case by either routing the edges or lining them with a molded face frame. A flat face frame or edge banding provides a more contemporary look.

FACE FRAMES The frames are made of strips of wood that are either flat or molded. The face frames can overhang the walls of the case by ¼ to 1 inch. First install your horizontal frames across the top and bottom of the case. The top edges of both the framing board and case should be flush. The top edge of the bottom board should be

flush with the top of the bottom shelf. Cut vertical frames to fit along the sides between the horizontal frames, making the outside

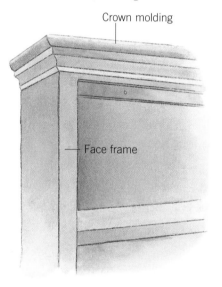

Crown molding

Face frame

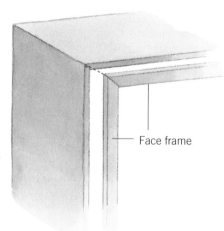

Face frame

edges of the frame flush with the outside of the case. The top of the case can be enhanced with a crown molding for added detail.

WOOD EDGING Thin strips of wood or trim applied to the front edges of the case and shelves will enhance and protect them. The wood should be the same width as the edges and can be applied with glue and finishing nails, using mitered joints at the corners. Consider using half-round or bead molding for a soft finish.

Wood edging

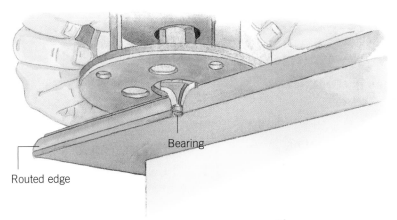

Routed edge
Bearing

ROUTED EDGES You can add decorative detail to the front edges of your case and shelves or limit the detail to the shelves themselves. In the latter case, you might want to run a face frame around the case and rout the shelf edges. To mold an edge, use a self-piloting router bit: Its bearing runs along the edge being shaped, guiding the router.

EDGE BANDING Use a thin plastic laminate tape to protect plywood or MDF. It comes in a range of colors, wood-grain patterns, and widths and can be ironed on to the edge of the case. Cut the banding a bit longer than needed, iron it in place, and trim the edges with a chisel or

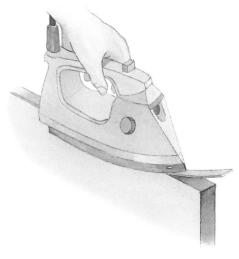

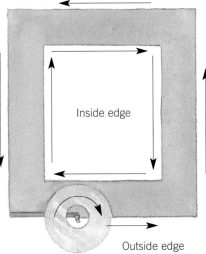

Inside edge

Outside edge

edge trimmer. Finish with a smooth file or 150-grit sandpaper.

SETTING NAILS, FILLING, SANDING, AND PAINTING

Once you've built your box or case, you will want to preserve it with some kind of protective coating. If you've used natural wood, you can apply a clear finish, stain, or paint. Plywood and MDF should be painted.

For the smoothest finish on your case or box, all nail heads should be set below the wood's surface using a nail set or countersink. Fill nail holes, dents, and other imperfec-

tions with wood filler, applying it with a putty knife or other flat tool. Larger gouges in the wood may require more than one application of filler, since many products shrink as they dry. When the filler is dry, sand the surface smooth.

STAINING If you are going to stain the wood, you may first want to apply a wood sealer. Softwoods absorb stain quickly and often unevenly; a sealer closes the wood pores and helps ensure an even finish. You can apply one or more coats of stain to achieve the color you want, sanding between applications. When the stain is dry, apply a finishing coat of polyurethane varnish or penetrating oil to protect the wood from fading or staining.

PAINTING If you want your cases to blend with your walls, match the color of your furniture, or provide a contrast to the rest of the room, use paint. Before painting, apply a coat of primer to all wood. Then apply one or two coats of paint as needed. Adjustable shelves should be painted before being inserted in the case. A semigloss or gloss paint—rather than one with a matte finish—will set the case apart from the walls and protect it from moisture damage.

resource guide

Once you have done the initial work of cleaning and sorting your possessions, keep your organizational strategy on track by purchasing the right storage products. Look for cabinets, closet systems, racks, and hardware from local home-improvement centers, such as The Home Depot, Lowe's, and Orchard Supply Hardware.

You will find storage furniture, containers, and accessories in abundance at retail stores, on the Internet, and through mail-order catalogs. A selection of specialty retailers, catalog companies, and manufacturers are listed here to help you get started with your search for storage products.

STORAGE AND ORGANIZATION PRODUCT RETAILERS

CALIFORNIA CLOSETS
1-888-336-9709
www.californiaclosets.com

THE CONTAINER STORE
1-888-266-8246
www.containerstore.com

HOLD EVERYTHING
1-800-421-2264
www.holdeverything.com

ORGANIZED LIVING
1-800-862-6556

ORGANIZE-EVERYTHING.COM
1-800-600-9817
www.organize-everything.com

ORGANIZE-IT
1-800-210-7712
www.organizes-it.com

STACKS AND STACKS HOMEWARES
1-800-761-5222
www.stacksandstacks.com

HOME FURNISHING RETAILERS

CRATE & BARREL
1-800-237-5672
www.crateandbarrel.com

IKEA
1-800-434-4532
www.ikea-usa.com

POTTERY BARN
1-800-922-5507
www.potterybarn.com

RESTORATION HARDWARE
1-800-816-0901
www.restorationhardware.com

ONLINE AND CATALOG RESOURCES

ARCHIVAL METHODS
1-866-877-7050
www.archivalmethods.com

BALLARD DESIGNS
1-800-367-2775
www.ballarddesigns.com

BERKELEY MILLS
1-510-549-2854
www.berkeleymills.com

COCOON
1-800-842-4352
www.cocoononline.com

DESIGN WITHIN REACH
1-800-944-2233
www.dwr.com

EASY TRACK
1-800-562-4257
www.easytrack.com

EXPOSURES
1-800-222-4947
www.exposuresonline.com

FRENCH COUNTRY LIVING
1-800-649-2314
www.frenchcountryliving.com

FRONTGATE
1-800-626-6488
www.frontgate.com

GEMPLER'S
1-800-382-8473
www.gemplers.com

GOOD CATALOG
www.goodcatalog.com

THE HOME MARKETPLACE
1-800-356-3876
www.thehomemarketplace.com

HYLOFT USA, LLC
1-866-249-5638
www.hyloftusa.com

IMPROVEMENTS
1-800-985-6044
www.improvementscatalog.com

THE MUSEUM OF MODERN ART
1-800-793-3167
www.moma.org

THE MUSEUM OF USEFUL THINGS STORE
1-800-515-2707
www.themut.com

PALOS SPORTS
1-800-233-5484
www.palossports.com

RACOR
1-800-783-7725
www.racorinc.com

SHARPER IMAGE
1-800-344-5555
www.sharperimage.com

SINCERELY YOURS
1-800-297-4860
www.sincerelyyours.com

SOLUTIONS
1-800-342-9988
www.solutionscatalog.com

CHILDREN'S RESOURCES
CHILDCRAFT
1-800-631-5652
www.childcraft.com

POTTERY BARN KIDS
1-800-430-7373
www.potterybarnkids.com

MEMBERSHIP WAREHOUSE CLUBS
COSTCO
1-800-774-2678
w w w . c o s t c o . c o m

SAM'S CLUB
1-800-925-6278
www.samsclub.com

WOODWORKING & HARDWARE RESOURCES
A BIG WAREHOUSE
1-480-926-5293
www.abigwarehouse.com

ROCKLER
1-800-279-4441
www.rockler.com

VAN DYKE'S RESTORERS
1-800-558-1234
www.vandykes.com

KITCHEN CABINET AND HARDWARE MANUFACTURERS & SUPPLIERS
BOWERY KITCHEN SUPPLY
1-212-376-4982
www.bowerykitchens.com

BULTHAUP KITCHEN ARCHITECHTURE
Los Angeles: 310-288-3875
Chicago: 312-787-9982
New York: 212-966-7183
www.bulthaup.com

HÄFELE
1-800-423-3531
www.hafeleonline.com/usa

KITCHEN ACCESSORIES UNLIMITED
1-800-667-8721
www.kitchenaccessoriesunlimited.com

KRAFTMAID
1-800-571-1990
www.kraftmaid.com

REAL SOLUTIONS FOR REAL LIFE BY KNAPE & VOGT
1-616-459-3311
www.knapeandvogt.com

REV-A-SHELF
1-800-626-1126
www.rev-a-shelf.com

RUBBERMAID
1-330-264-6464
1-888-895-2110
www.rubbermaid.com

SIEMATIC
1-800-559-0793
www.siematic.com

ACKNOWLEDGEMENTS
We would like to thank the following people and businesses for their assistance: Fray Below; Thomas Blaine; Carrie Bowman, Knape & Vogt; Bulthaup; Keri Butler, Rubbermaid; Amy Crowley, Frontgate; Lois Erbay, California Closets; Exposures; Frank Gaglione; Bette Johnson, Windquest Companies Inc.; Amy Kirkbride, Knape & Vogt; the library staff at SPC Picture Collection; Tim Matthias, HyLoft USA, LLC; Joan Perniconi, Crate & Barrel; Diane Rock, Rev-A-Shelf; Jan Schlesinger, California Closets; Debbie Schwartz, The Village Collection Inc.; Janice Simonsen, IKEA; Marion and Fred Sotcher; Thomas J. Story; Kelly Vrtis, The Container Store.

PHOTOGRAPHERS
Jean Allsopp/SPC Picture Collection: 72 left; **Dennis Anderson:** 56 bottom right; **Ron Anderson:** 59 top left; **Laurie Black:** 14 right, 128 bottom left and right; **Marion Brenner:** 172 top right; **Caroline Bureau, Robert Chartier, Michel Thibault:** 186; **Ed Caldwell:** 109 right; **James Carrier:** 2 bottom left, 33 bottom right, 62 top, 112 bottom right, 138; **Ken Chen:** 157 top right; **Crandall & Crandall:** 74 top, 168 top and bottom right; **Crate & Barrel/James Baigrie:** 33 top right, 134 left; **Crate & Barrel/Steven McDonald:** 75 top right; **Crate & Barrel/Simon Watson:** 36 bottom left; 51 bottom right, 126 top; **Crate & Barrel/Gintas Zaranka:** 134 bottom; **Grey Crawford:** 63 top right; **Alan & Linda Detrick:** 171 left, bottom right; **Kevin Dwarka:** 109 left; **Derek Fell:** 170 bottom right, 171 top right; **Frank Gaglione:** 2 bottom right, 6 left, 7 left, 24, 25 all, 40, 41 all, 66, 67 all, 92, 93 all, 99 left, 114, 115 all, 129 bottom, 136, 137 all, 150, 160, 161 all, 174, 175 all, 178, 179 all; **Dana Gallagher:** 15 top right; **Getty Images (copyright © 2003):** 20 left; **Tria Giovan:** 3 top left, 16, 33 left, 46 top, 48, 59 bottom left, 65 left, 95 bottom left, 113 top, 117 top, 119 left; **Jay Graham:** 51 top, 60 bottom right, 61 left, 70 top right, 103 bottom, 129 top; **John Granen:** 116 top, 119 top right, 130 left, 139, 140 top right; **Ken Gutmaker:** 23 left, 71 bottom right, 81 right, 95 bottom right, 140 bottom right; **Jamie Hadley:** 11 bottom right, 57 left, 63 bottom right, 95 top; **Margot Hartford:** 18 top right, 26 left; **Philip Harvey:** 14 bottom center, 72 top right, 73 top right, 128 top left, 133 bottom left, 143 left; **Alex Hayden:** 27 all; **Michael Jensen:** 65 top right; **Douglas Johnson:** 108 left;

Steve Keating: 112 bottom left; **Muffy Kibbey:** 15 top left and center, 116 bottom right, 144 left; **Dennis Krukowski:** 118 bottom; **David Duncan Livingston:** 59 top right, 73 left, 142 right, 147 left; **Janet Loughrey:** 172 left, 176 top; **Kathryn MacDonald:** 74 bottom; **Peter Malinowski/ InSite:** 58 right, 146 left; **Dave Marlow:** 108 right; **Sylvia Martin/SPC Photo Collection:** 34 bottom right; **E. Andrew McKinney:** 37 bottom right, 80 left, 97 all, 102, 104 top right, 105 left, 124 bottom, 127 bottom, 176 bottom, 180, 184 top; **Susan Gentry McWhinney:** 2 top right, 11 bottom left, 12 left, 82, 91 top; **Art Meripol/SPC Picture Collection:** 81 top left; **Miller/Stein Design:** 70 left; **Kit Morris:** 42 top right, 75 left, 118 top right; **Wendy Nordeck:** 117 bottom; **David Papazian:** 64 top left, 125 top; **David Phelps:** 49 bottom left; **Norman A. Plate:** 56 left, 162 bottom right; **David Prince:** 3 middle right, 4, 5 bottom right, 7 right, 12 right, 13 right, 20 top and bottom right, 50 right, 81 bottom left, 89 top right, 120 right, 121 top, 122, 126 bottom, 133 right, 134 top right, 135 bottom left, 144 top right; **Tom Rider:** 9 left, 53, 148 bottom right; **Michael Shopenn:** 26 right; **Brad Simmons/Beateworks.com:** 11 top right, 17; **Michael Skott:** 1, 2 top left, 3 bottom left, 9 bottom right, 22 right, 23 bottom right, 31 bottom right, 32 left, 36 top left, 37 left and top right, 38 right, 46 bottom, 49 top, 52, 57 bottom right, 62 bottom, 75 bottom right, 119 bottom right, 130 right, 148 left, 166, 189; **Janet Sorrell/ The Garden Picture Library:** 167; **Thomas J. Story:** 3 middle left, 15 bottom right, 18 left, 19 center, 22 left, 23 top right, 39, 44 bottom, 47, 50 bottom left, 61 top right, 76 all, 77 top and bottom left, 78, 80 top and bottom right, 91 bottom left, 103 top left, 104 left and bottom right, 105 bottom right, 106, 110 right, 112 top, 113 bottom, 118 left, 120 left, 131 top and bottom left, 133 top left, 141 top and bottom left, 145 right, 152 left, 154 left, 155 left, 158 all, 159 all, 162 left and top right, 164 top, 165, 170 left and top right, 172 bottom right, 177 bottom left; **Tim Street-Porter:** 65 bottom right, 99 top right; **Tim Street-Porter/Beateworks.com:** 8 left, 14 top center, 29, 30 bottom, 54, 60 left, 63 left; **John Sutton:** 15 bottom left; **Luca Trovato:** 5 left, 5 top right, 6 left, 86 right, 89 top left, 188; **Brian Vanden Brink:** 10 right, 21, 31 top right, 36 right, 42 bottom right, 49 bottom right, 64 right, 83, 91 bottom right, 132 left, 135 bottom right, 140 left, 145 left, 146 right, 148 top right, 151, 164 bottom; **Christopher Vendetta:** 182, 184 bottom; **Michal Venera:** 3 top right, 18 bottom right, 19 top right, 28, 30 top, 31 left, 34 left, 51 bottom left, 107, 110 left, 125 bottom left, 142 left; **Jessie Walker:** 9 top right, 58 top left, 71 bottom left, 90 right; **David Wakely:** 38 left, 42 left, 57 top right, 59 bottom right, 61 bottom right, 70 bottom right, 94 top, 121 bottom, 124 top, 128 top right, 143 right, 147 right; **Rick Wetherbee:** 14 left; **Peter O. Whiteley:** 173; **Ben Woolsey:** 71 top right

ARCHITECTS & DESIGNERS

Andre Rothblatt Architecture: 71 bottom right, 81 right, 140 bottom right; **Arkin-Tilt Architects:** 109 top right; **Associates III/Cottle Graybeal Yaw Architects:** 108 right; **Patricia Bainter:** 57 top right; **Lou Ann Bauer:** 14 bottom center; **Bernhard & Priestly Architects:** 42 bottom right; **Michael Bliss & Chris Jacobson/ Gardenart:** 172 bottom right; **Obie Bowman:** 9 left, 148 bottom right; **BurksToma Architects, Marie Fisher Interior Design, Min/Day:** 60 bottom right; **C. David Robinson Architects:** 15 center, 110 right; **Debi Cekosh/Cekosh Design Studio & Michael Gibson Architectural Design:** 147 left; **Susan Christman:** 71 top right; **City Building, Inc:** 73 top right; **Butch Cleveland:** 157 top right; **David Coleman:** 14 right; **Custom Electronics Designers:** 31 top right; **Nancy Cowall Cutler:** 80 left; **Malcolm Davis:** 74 bottom; **Don Del Fava:** 177 bottom left; **Mark De Mattei/Terry Martin/Patricia McDonald/Marcia Moore:** 14 top left; **Jean-Louis Deniot:** 65 bottom right; **Kirsten Dumo/Satterberg Desonier Dumo Interior Design:** 139; **Donham & Sweeny Architects:** 91 bottom right; **Sasha Dunn:** 3 middle right, 4, 5 bottom right, 7 right, 12 right, 13 right, 20 top and bottom right, 50 right, 81 bottom left, 89 top right, 120 right, 121 top, 122, 126 bottom, 133 right, 134 top right, 135 bottom left; **144 top right; **Mark Dutka/InHouse:** 124 bottom; **Michele Dutra/Custom Kitchens by John Wilkins:** 61 left; 103 bottom; **Elliott & Elliott Architects:** 140 left; **Heidi M. Emmett:** 127 bottom; **Steve Fidrych:** 172 top right; **Claudia Fleury/Claudia's Designs:** 23 left; **Bill Galli/ Melissa Griggs:** 95 bottom right; **John Gillespie:** 132 left; **Bret Hancock/Thatcher & Thompson Architects:** 155 left; **Holly Opfelt Design:** 97 bottom; **Mark Horton:** 63 bottom right; **House + House Architects:** 33 bottom right; **Jann Jaffe/Garden Lane Floral:** 146 left; **Jayne Sanders Interior Design:** 141 bottom left; **Steve Keating/Designs Northwest Architects:** 112 bottom left; **Little Folk Art/Susan Salzman:** 104 top right; **Ronald W. Madson/Madson Associates:** 26 left; **Mark Hutker & Associates Architects:** 83, 148 top right; **Miles Clay Designs:** 58 right; **Marcia Miller and Steven Stein, Miller/Stein Design:** 70 left; **Freddy Moran/Carlene Anderson Kitchen Design:** 37 bottom right; **Morningstar Marble & Granite:** 64 right; **Jodi Murphy:** 11 bottom right; **Dan Nelson/Designs Northwest Architects:** 27 right; **Markie Nelson Interior Design:** 130 left, 140 top right; **Kevin Patrick O'Brien & Janice Stone Thomas:** 61 bottom right, 128 top right, 143 right, 147 right; **Christine Oliver:** 145 left; **Jim O'Neill/OZ Architects:** 70 bottom right; **Osburn Design:** 128 top left; **Wendy Nordeck/ Levy Art & Architecture and Sandra Slater/ Environments:** 117 bottom; **Wayne Palmer:** 42 left, 121 bottom; **Pamela Pennington Studios:** 15 center, 105 bottom right, 110 right; 116 bottom right, 144 left; **Kit Parmentier/Allison Rose:** 95 top; **David Pelletier/Pelletier + Schaar for Designs Northwest:** 27 left; **Plan One:** 116 top; **Prentiss Architects:** 65 top right; **Arne and Sandra Reyier:** 71 right; **Heidi Richardson:** 56 left; **Sagstuen Design:** 59 bottom right, 124 top; **Steven W. Sanborn:** 143 left; **Sandra Bird Custom Kitchens:** 56 bottom right; **Sant Architects:** 63 top right; **Paul Scardina:** 128 bottom left and right; **Scholz & Barclay Architects:** 146 right; **SkB Architects:** 119 top right; **D. Kimberly Smith/Deer Creek Design:** 102; **Dick Stennick:** 18 top right; **Henry Taylor:** 53; **Diana and Shawn Tibor:** 173; **Robert and Nancy Tiner:** 176 bottom; **Debra S. Weiss:** 97 top, 105 left; **Weston & Hewitson Architects:** 10 right, 36 right, 49 bottom right; **Henry Wood:** 109 top left; **Charles Wooldridge:** 26 right; **José Vilar/Rebecca Hayden:** 38 left; **Zack/de Vito Architecture:** 109 bottom left

RETAILERS & MANUFACTURERS

We would like to thank the following retailers and manufacturers for giving us permission to feature their photography: **Bulthaup:** 56 top right, 72 bottom right; **California Closets (© 2003 California Closets Company/All Rights Reserved):** 84 left, 88 left and top right, 89 bottom right, 98 top, 123, 149 left, 156 left, 157 bottom right; **The Container Store:** 10 left, 32 right, 44 top, 45, 77 bottom right, 77 middle and bottom right, 79 top, 86 left, 87, 89 bottom left, 96 right, 98 bottom, 131 top right, 132 top and bottom right, 149 right, 152 right, 153, 154 right; **Crate & Barrel/James Baigrie:** 33 stop right, 134 left; **Crate & Barrel/Steven McDonald:** 75 top right; **Crate & Barrel/Simon Watson:** 36 bottom left; 51 bottom right, 126 top; **Crate & Barrel/Gintas Zaranka:** 134 bottom; **Easy Track/Racor:** 155 right, 156 right; **Exposures:** 8 right, 13 top and bottom left, 43 right, 103 top right, 135 top right; **Frontgate:** 73 bottom right, 157 left; **Hyloft USA:** 163; **IKEA:** 34 top right, 35 all, 50 top left, 58 bottom left, 84 right, 85, 88 bottom right, 90 left, 94 bottom, 96 left, 99 bottom right, 105 top right, 111, 116 bottom left, 127 top, 135 top center, 141 right, 144 bottom right; **Pottery Barn:** 3 top right, 18 bottom right, 19 top right, 28, 30 top, 31 left, 34 left, 51 bottom left, 107, 110 left, 125 bottom left, 142 left; **Real Solutions for Real Life:** 60 top right, 64 bottom left; **Rev-A-Shelf:** 79 bottom; **Rubbermaid:** 168 left, 169, 177 right and top left.

index